DATE

D1550355

Pony Trekking

Pony trekking offers the ideal holiday in the open air for those who want group activity in close conjunction with animals and the countryside. Edward Hart shows that trekking is immensely rewarding for families, friends, and individuals; a splendid opportunity for every town-dweller to learn the rudiments of horsemanship in open country. This is also a book for every lover of ponies, providing a guide to their requirements, stamina, equipment, and even their language, while describing the different characteristics of the breeds.

Widen Your Horizons with this new series

Remember that we cater for all interests. See for yourself with our expanding list of titles.

Places to see

Scottish Islands — Tom Weir
Dartmoor — Crispin Gill

Leisure activities

Railways for Pleasure — Geoffrey Body
Good Photography Made Easy — Derek Watkins
Looking at Churches — David Bowen

Sporting

The Art of Good Shooting — J. E. M. Ruffer
Archery for All — Daniel Roberts

Holidays

Canoe Touring — Noel McNaught

Forthcoming titles

Exmoor — Colin Jones
Sea Fishing for Fun — Alan Wrangles
A Guide to Safe Rock Climbing — Patrick Scrivenor
Rowing for Everyone — Christopher Chant

Pony Trekking

Edward Hart

David & Charles
Newton Abbot   London
North Pomfret (VT)   Vancouver

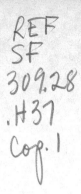

ISBN 0 7153 7242 4
Library of Congress Catalog Card Number 76–8623

© Edward Hart 1976.

Set in 11 on 13 Bembo
and printed in Great Britain
by Redwood Burn Limited, Trowbridge and Esher
for David & Charles (Publishers) Limited
Brunel House   Newton Abbot   Devon

Published in the United States of America
by David & Charles Inc
North Pomfret   Vermont 05053   USA

Published in Canada
by Douglas David & Charles Limited
1875 Welch Street   North Vancouver   BC

Contents

1 Why go Pony Trekking?

'Change is the key' said Sir Winston Churchill on leisure activities. Pony trekking offers the complete change from everyday life for the majority. Instead of the machine or typewriter, you deal with an animal. Office or factory walls are replaced by hills and sky. An unchanging environment at work becomes a constantly varying succession of different fields, moors, woods and cloud formations, backcloth to equine and human companionship.

A common interest is the mainspring of new friendships. Your horse, his idiosyncrasies, speed, colour or breeding rightly become the most important things in life, as they have been to generations of horsemen before you. You become one of them. No longer are you on the outside. You will discover that in truth the best thing for the inside of a man is the outside of a horse.

Though previous experience is an advantage, it is by no means essential. A number of beginners are to be found at every trekking centre, and if you know little of horses at the beginning, you will have more than a smattering at the end. Above all, it is great fun. Just as horses behave better in a herd, so humans learn more easily among others in the same position. Instructors are usually competent and pleasant, otherwise they would not be there. A number of girls have met their future husbands at trekking centres!

The main essentials for a pony trekking holiday are average physical fitness and a spirit of adventure. If you mind getting wet through, don't go. If your own meal is more important to you than your horse's, find another holiday. There is no age limit, and quite young children find the average trek within their capabilities. For experienced riders only, 'riding holidays' are arranged at various centres, where the pace is faster and you can often take your own mount.

On most treks, the usual pace is the walk. An occasional trot or canter relieves saddle pressure on the pony's back, and increases the rider's circulation rate on a cold day, but in general the walk predominates. This progress makes trekking eminently suitable for the

Pony trekking comes to town. This Edinburgh parade marks the tenth anniversary of the sport in 1962. The predominant breed here is Highland, as would be expected in Scotland

beginner; the object is not to get from A to B in the shortest possible time, but to enjoy the journey and absorb the happenings of the countryside while doing so.

Trekking is seasonal, except at one or two centres open all the year round. It usually begins in mid-April to include Easter, and ends in late September or October. Riding holidays are available throughout the year. They include visits to shows and gymkhanas, with the possibility of evening films and lectures. The north and west offer more trekking facilities than the Home Counties, simply because drove roads, mountains and moorland are more suited to trekking than land under intensive agriculture. At all times, remember that you are moving over someone's business premises, whether they be sheep and grouse moors, forest, or enclosed fields. All land in Britain, even common land, belongs to someone, and though there are many rights of way, tidiness and observance of the Country Code are the start of good manners.

7

Where hotels are combined with trekking, excellent value for money is obtained. Because of the extra business which trekking brings to hotels, they are often able to offer inclusive prices which are little more than is paid by ordinary residents. There is the additional bonus of entertainment on the spot. Some hotels hold a dance several times a week, and this is free; you don't have to travel miles and buy an expensive ticket, but swing around to pleasant music in a room bedecked with coaching prints, horse brasses and shoes, with horse models and bridles on the walls.

Social activities and dances are never more enjoyable than after a day in the open. Following hours of wind, rain or sun the ponies are attended to, and then it is your turn. A hot bath, a change out of riding gear into something smart, and you're all set for the evening. Here is the element of contrast, of hot dining hall dinner after a midday packed lunch by the banks of a tinkling stream, with hobbled horses shaking themselves and grazing nearby. Comfort after activity: that is the stuff of trekking. Post trekking (see Chapter 8) may be at a disadvantage in this respect, and is only recommended if you prefer the hard life the whole time, though some post trekkers stay at hotels.

If the weekly rate is well below average, either ponies, saddlery or accommodation is not up to standard. Shortcomings on any of these points ruins a holiday. Ill-fitting saddles are a common cause of back trouble, and put the pony out of action more often than any other mishap. Good saddles are expensive. Girths are not, but a weak girth is highly dangerous, leading to loss of confidence in any young rider without the experience to notice a defect that should not have been

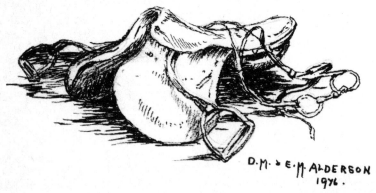

D.M. & E.M. ALDERSON
1976.

there. Again, pay a reasonable price, and expect pony, tack, food and beds to be up to the mark.

Stiff and sore after using unaccustomed muscles, you are well on the way to becoming an accomplished horseman or horsewoman if you can still put your mount's needs first though tired, cold and hungry yourself.

During the evenings you will amass much horse lore, some of it exaggerated, but all fascinating. Once bitten by the trekking bug, you discover how vast is the world of the horse, how endless and infinite its attractions, how many volumes since the earliest Greeks, and drawings from the time of primitive man, have been devoted to it. Few human conditions have given greater lasting pleasure than love of horses.

As Churchill also said: 'No hour of life is lost which is spent in the saddle'.

2 Introducing the Pony

'Pony trekking' has become an accepted phrase in the English language. It owes its origin to a young South African doctor, Ronnie Wylde, who won the Empire Games 440 yards Championships in 1938. Later he coached athletes in Scotland, and frequently sang a number of Afrikaans trekking songs. At the time J. Kerr Hunter was searching for a name for a newly-pioneered riding venture. 'I found myself humming the song *Sarie Marais.* Suddenly I had it. "Trekking!" I said. "Pony trekking – that's it", and everyone agreed. There was a lilt of adventure about it and a feeling of wide open spaces.'

This was in 1952, when Ewan Ormiston put all his faith and capital into the idea. Like many others he was desperately seeking a way of preventing native British breeds of ponies from disappearing from the scene and being replaced by a haze of petrol fumes. He seized on J. Kerr Hunter's trekking idea and the first centre was set up at Newtonmore, Inverness-shire. It was fitting that Highland ponies were the means of introducing pony trekking; they had been used with great success by the Scottish Horse in the Boer War, and Ormiston's stud of Highland ponies formed a vital nucleus.

'He may not have known he was leading a crusade for a better deal for the native ponies of Scotland, but he most certainly led it, and hundreds of ponies now living might have ended up as meals for dogs or their human masters if he had not made trekking fashionable', wrote Hunter ten years later.

Since 1952 at least as many ponies have been born which, had it not been for trekking, would never even have been conceived. So when you go on a trekking holiday, you not only enjoy yourself but give added impetus to pony breeding.

In 1954 Hugh MacGregor started the Aberfoyle centre. It is noteworthy that these two pioneering ventures are still flourishing, and that basic codes of conduct laid down by such professional horsemen have needed little change since.

Highland ponies in the film *Kidnapped*, shot in Glencoe. These ponies belong to Hugh MacGregor's Aberfoyle centre, and are used for trekking as well as film work

Pony Breeds

There is no 'best' breed of pony for trekking. Britain is fortunate in having nine native mountain and moorland breeds, each of which has been developed regionally to cope with its local environment. Most of them may be adapted to any part of the country, and offer a range suitable for a small child and a heavy man. In geographical order, beginning in the south-west, these breeds are Dartmoor, Exmoor, New Forest, Welsh, Fell, Dales, Highland, Shetland, and the Connemara from Ireland.

The Shetland Pony

For very small children the Shetland is an obvious starting point. In his classic *The Horse*, 1831, Youatt described this pony as 'often

exceedingly beautiful, with a small head, good-tempered countenance, a short neck, shoulders low and thick – in so little a creature far from being a blemish – legs flat and fine, and pretty round feet'. As the only British pony below ten hands, the Shetland has very much more endurance than the youngsters small enough to ride him. If he is not included in the trekking squad, it is because distances are too far for juvenile riders, not for the pony. One of them, nine hands (3 feet) in height, carried a 12-stone man 40 miles in one day.

The 'Sheltie' is usually dark brown or black, but there are a number of attractive greys and piebalds. Its Stud Book began in 1890, but its history reaches back to very early times, as ancient sculptured stones on its native islands prove. The small size is inherent, and in no way a degeneracy. One disadvantage of the Shetland on a trek is that when the string of ponies turns for home, strides lengthen, and only the exceptional Shetland can keep up with the rest without breaking into a trot. Obviously this is undesirable with so small a rider.

Dartmoor and Exmoor

Britain's two south-western breeds are Dartmoor and Exmoor. Both are comparatively small, but very tough. Dartmoors attract lady breeders, as a visit to shows with breed classes will confirm. Maximum height is 12.2 hands for both mares and stallions, and colours are bay, brown, black, grey and chestnut. However, no colours are barred except piebald and skewbald. The head is small, with good eyes and small, alert ears. Fine riding action comes from very good riding shoulders, while legs have medium bone and sound, strong feet. 'Tail is well set up and full', says the breed standard.

In 1831 Youatt wrote: 'There is on Dartmoor a race of ponies much in request in that vicinity, being sure-footed and hardy, and admirably calculated to scramble over the rough roads and dreary wilds of that mountainous district. The Dartmoor pony is larger than the Exmoor, and, if possible, uglier.'

The sure-footedness remains, but the ugliness has been completely fined out in the intervening century and a half. The Dartmoor stallion Hilsey Woodcock, foaled in 1962, was several times Supreme Champion Mountain and Moorland Stallion. Although the breed's main centres are in the south-west, it has spread to all parts of Britain, gaining followers every year.

White Shetland Pony

Scenes like this take on new meaning to pony trekkers. Now part of the world of horses, you really appreciate the wheelings and dealings at Appleby Fair, Cumbria, each June. Few can resist a Shetland foal, especially a piebald

Early last century a governor of Dartmoor Prison coveted one of the near-wild ponies in the vicinity. He and several men separated it from the herd, and drove it on some rocks by the side of a tor (an abrupt pointed hill). The little animal jumped completely over a mounted man sent to capture it, and escaped. This is the agility that has been retained.

'There is a brown colour with a mealy nose and flanks that is said to predominate on Exmoor, and this is also very strongly prepotent when Exmoors are mated with other breeds', said *Standard Cyclopedia of Modern Agriculture*.

This mealy nose is worth looking for in ponies of your string, or those passed by the wayside. Mealy markings are also found round the eyes and inside flanks. There should be no white anywhere. The main point about the Exmoor pony is that a fit and mature pure-bred animal can and will carry 12 stone all day, and is remarkably cheap to maintain. An indication of the great suitability of these two breeds for

Dartmoor pony

trekking is their former use as pack animals. Larger sorts of Dartmoors and Exmoors were used to carry hay, corn, dung, fuel, stones and lime – in fact everything for farm or household, for early last century there were farms in the area on which there was not a pair of wheels. Bred from animals used to such burdens along the roughest tracks, the modern Exmoor and Dartmoor remain excellent for human burdens.

You can tell if your pony is a true Exmoor, for he will have the Society's star and his herd number on the near shoulder. On the near flank he will carry his individual number. He therefore carries his pedigree on his tough hide. Only the best receive this accolade, as they are rounded up each autumn and examined by Society inspectors. Thus if you buy a branded Exmoor at any age or in any place, the Society will tell you his herd, his breeding, and his original owner. The native Exmoor is brought up in a hard country, and keeps his hardiness and intelligence even though he goes to kinder climates.

Welsh Ponies: Ideal for Trekking

Welsh ponies offer the complete range. They are classified according to height into Sections A, B, C, and D. Section A is for Welsh Mountain ponies not exceeding 12 hands; B is for Welsh ponies not exceeding 13.2 hands; C for Welsh ponies (cob type) not exceeding 13.2 hands; D for Welsh cobs, with E for geldings.

Properly-bred Welsh ponies make ideal trekkers. At some centres in the Principality, the Welsh is used exclusively, traditional types being best for trekking. By this I mean the strong-boned, 'sensible' pony used for shepherding, not the fine-boned, fine-headed type with a dash of Arab or Thoroughbred blood which has found favour with certain judges. 'The old sort', as its devotees term it, is still widely found, and its wonderful characteristics are jealously guarded.

A good Welsh pony, like an Exmoor, will carry a man all day on the hill. This it has done for generations, in all weathers, and far from tracks. The Welsh shepherding pony has been bred to carry a sheep as well, so it is unlikely to be upset by trekking routine. You cannot

Black Dizzy, the Welsh Cob (*left*) was believed to be the last surviving horse to serve in World War II. He was used by the Forces as a pack horse, before becoming a trek animal. His companion also shows plenty of bone and substance

know what type of Welsh is kept until you reach your centre, except by verification from other guests that the ponies are indeed those you seek. Most centres avoid the rather flighty, very fine-boned show types as unsuitable for novice riders anyway.

Any colour except piebald and skewbald is acceptable in the Welsh. The Section B pony is described in the Welsh Pony and Cob Society Stud Book as 'a riding pony, with quality, riding action, adequate bone and substance, hardiness and constitution and with pony character'.

Lucky is the rider of a Welsh cob. This animal was selected over the years to do every job on the farm, to take the farmer to market, the family to church or chapel on Sunday in a trap, or son or daughter to the next farm in the saddle. Fortunately, though numbers declined with the coming of the motor car, original strains have been retained. Inevitably some crossing occurred, both with cart and hackney stallions, and not every Welsh cob is of the true old-fashioned strains, but in general they are excellent trek animals. A cob normally has shorter legs in proportion to its height, compared with larger riding horses. It should be strong, hardy and active, with pony character and as much substance as possible. Coarse head and Roman nose are most

Welsh cob

It's not trekking weather, but these hardy Welsh ponies live on the mountain summer and winter alike. Studs of this size, with stallion running with the mares, are a feature of the Principality. This scene is above Llangollen, North Wales

objectionable, says the Society. Action should be free, true and forcible. Those who watched that wonderful cob stallion flicking his heels at the 1975 Horse of the Year Show need no reminding that here indeed is a master performer.

Some years ago a leading cob breeder wrote:

'There is something infinitely fascinating about the speedy, hardy, metalled, old-world trotting Cob of Wales – and much that savours of romance about its history. That as a sane and eminently useful equine proposition it is the very envy of the world is demonstrated by the long-established and enduring fame which it enjoys throughout these islands, and by the ever-growing call for it overseas.'

From the New Forest

Most of us have read Captain Marryat's *Children of the New Forest*. This gives an excellent idea of the general-purpose nature of the New Forest pony in its early days. Billy the pony did his share on the farm and as saddle horse. Ponies ran wild in the New Forest, and catching them was, according to Youatt, 'as great a trial of skill as the hunting of the wild horse on the Pampas of South America, and a greater one of patience'.

Welsh mountain stallion

New Forest ponies

The native stock was influenced by a succession of Thoroughbred and Arab stallions at varying intervals. Each wrought an improvement, but the commoners of those days sold the best, thus leaving the worst for breeding. This process continued until the next improver came along. Most notable were Marske, sire of the famous racehorse Eclipse, who spent at least four years in the Forest before being traced as an outstanding sire, and some Rhum ponies. These were the original black Galloways bought by Lord Arther Cecil in 1888. Remote islands are ideal for keeping stock pure, and the Rhum ponies had one curious characteristic. Their eyes were always hazel, not brown. This trait is worth noting, for the back-breeding of any ponies seen today with hazel eyes would be most interesting.

The modern New Forest is a large pony, up to 14.2 hands. It occurs in a variety of whole colours; at the 1975 Royal Show were bays, browns, chestnuts, blacks, greys and grey/duns. Among their ancestors were ponies that could trot 12 miles in 55 minutes after they were 20 years old, a good enough basis on which to base any trekking pony.

In the Forest some 3,000 ponies run with about 120 stallions. All stallions must be registered in the Stud Book, have a veterinary certificate for soundness, and be passed as of suitable type. All are branded after the foal stage. There are 925 registered brands, most ponies being branded on the left saddle, some on the left shoulder, and

Dales ponies at Stoneriggs, Appleby (Cumbria), Britain's largest stud of the breed. Some of this strain have 'mane a yard long' as favoured by former breeders. The Dales' hairy fetlocks are a protection against wet conditions. Giving a titbit when walking among ponies helps make them easy to catch

others on the left hip or in two places. These brands are in the form of initials – R, HD, RA and DD being well known. No outside blood has been introduced since the mid 1930s.

Adaptability is a strong New Forest trait. Prince Andrew learnt to drive with the ponies Garth Remus and Deeracres Sally. Beelzebub of Ramblers won a Bronze Horse Shoe in the BHS Long Distance Ride of 75 miles, averaging 8 miles an hour against horses several inches taller.

Dales and Fell Ponies

From the north of England come two excellent trekking breeds, the Dales and the Fell. From the same basic Pennine and Lakeland stock, these ponies are predominantly black or dark-brown, with no white except a star, or a patch on the hind feet. There are a few greys, but Fells include bays, sometimes seen with black points and very attractive indeed.

These ponies have power. If you are on the heavy side, a Dales or

Fell will still take you anywhere. A Weardale (County Durham) farmer scales 15 stone, yet his Fell pony takes him round the quarry faces which constitute much of his upland acreage. The Fell is limited to 14 hands, the Dales to 14.2.

Trekking is merely a variation of the job for which these northcountry breeds were moulded generation after generation. Mr John Wall of Bradford recalled their practical use as pack animals. 'Fell ponies used to carry lead from the mines, pannier fashion, eight stones a side, and walked 240 miles a week to the docks at Tyneside'. The dead weight of lead is far more burdensome than the veriest beginner at riding. Special wooden saddles were constructed to carry ore from mines to smelting works, and coal was taken in the same way to lonely farmsteads.

Despite the weights carried, a clean, straight and true action has been developed. Dales ponies have trotted a mile in 3 minutes, and there is one stallion on a northern farm that is never fully extended in the show ring though 18 years old, simply because no man can keep up with him at the trot in the in-hand classes.

'The Dales pony should display the true pony character, alertness, strength and substance. Energy, yet docility, and the hardiness of the true Mountain and Moorland pony'. Thus states the Dales Pony Society, stressing another breed characteristic, flowing, long mane. 'Mane a yard long' was indeed an ideal of older breeders, and ponies of this type are still found today. Not for such men the clean legs, fine mane and light bone that typify mixed show ring classes. Mane and tail give protection against a dales winter, hairy fetlocks keep an animal warmer in wet, squelchy conditions. As these ponies invariably winter out, they must have weatherproof coats, and the shelter of a stone wall or thorn bush under the hill is all they ask. They keep their condition where a cross-bred animal would die.

Dales and Fells are admirable ride-and-drive animals. They are adept at hauling sledges of hay to outlying flocks in severe storm, so there is no reason to fear their endurance on a summer trek. At the walk they are unbeatable, and this combined with their ability to live cheaply makes them great favourites at trekking establishments. Their temperament is seldom remarked, because it is universally good.

Big is Best

There is much to be said for a large pony, for any except very small children. The stride is longer, giving a more comfortable and relaxing ride at the walk. This longer stride is easier for the novice. You have more pony in front and behind; if a small pony puts its head down, there is little to stop you going over its neck. If its rider tips off a Dales or Fell, the mount is unlikely to wander away more than a few yards, whereas a half-bred pony might immediately set off for home.

The large pony is much less liable to break down. Leg and foot muscles are stronger, and it is very uncommon for a Dales or Fell to have trouble in those parts. Cross-bred, light-legged ponies are much more liable to strains.

Children noticeably aim at a bigger pony if they begin on a small one. They never wish to return to the smaller size. The natural pace of the Dales and Fell is the walk, and if they are induced into a canter, they usually only keep it up for 20 or 30 yards, which is far enough for a novice. They maintain condition even on rough grazing, and so are less likely to get sore backs or girth galls, than thin ponies.

The Dales and Fell take life very easily, and seldom sweat even on

Fell pony

the hottest summer day. Their thick winter coats have one disadvantage, however. October weather may be still warm, and after a trek the horses go into the stable dry, then sweat because of their heavy hair. A chill may then ensue, and for this reason October trekking is not always practised.

The Highland Pony

As the Fell and Dales were bred to carry coal and ore, so the Highland pony was developed to bring a heavy stag down from the hill on its back, and for all farm tasks. A true weight-carrying pony may not be the most comfortable swift ride, but that does not concern us. We want a pony to carry us safely and surely at the walk, keeping us clear of bog, hole and rock, and this the Highland does from birth in its natural surroundings.

A great advantage of the breed is its big variation in size as well as colour. This makes it very suitable for a trekking centre, as all sizes of people may be carried. While the Highland Pony Society controls official height for registrations at 14.2 hands, there are a number of ponies that reach 15 hands, and obviously these are invaluable for heavyweight riders. We must remember that while a 14 hands pony

Highland pony

will carry a big weight occasionally, as in deer stalking, to do so week after week for full days, up and down hill, is a totally different matter. No pony should be asked to carry more than it can comfortably manage. An experienced trekking operator knows at a glance if the pony is overloaded, or the rider underhorsed.

Any whole colour is allowed by the Highland Pony Society. Black, brown, various shades of dun or grey, or fox colour with silver mane and tail are all correct for the breed. The eel stripe along the back is a typical feature, but is not always present. Height is 13 hands to 14.2 hands. The back should be short, with slight natural curve, the quarters and loins powerful, with tail strong, well set on and carried gaily, with a plentiful covering of hair reaching almost to the ground. A good Highland has the ideal pony head; well carried, attractive and broad between bright and kindly eyes, short between eyes and muzzle, with wide nostrils and short, well set ears. Viewed in profile, the breadth rather than the length of head and jawbone should be pronounced. The Highland's neck should be strong and not short, with arched crest and flowing mane. There you have the centrepiece of many a Highland painting and poem. Burns wrote:

'I paint thee out a Highland filly,
A sturdy, stubborn, handsome dapple,
As sleek's a mouse, as round's an apple.'

Docility is a common characteristic of this pony. An unbroken youngster named Mist was so placid that after being ridden on the leading rein by a young girl, she was ridden free for an hour. She was shod a day or two later and went immediately to the moor, where she not only carried down a heavy stag but hauled two hinds by the saddle breast straps, in a difficult place where no pony had been for 30 years. Mist had been handled regularly since she was a foal, but inherent placidity is needed for a young horse to be pressed into service in emergency, as was the case here.

One well-known stud is all descended from a single mare, a testimony to regular breeding. Highland ponies may, like Highland cattle, be named in the Gaelic; Ros Dhu, Calliach Bhan, Bennachie, and An Righ Muir are examples, and what better name than Woodbeer Tam O'Shanter for a gelding?

The Rev Mr Hall (*Travels in Scotland*), quoted by Youatt, wrote: 'When these animals [Highland ponies] come to any boggy piece of ground, they first put their nose on it, and then pat on it in a peculiar way with one of their forefeet; and from the sound and feel of the ground, they know whether it will bear them. They do the same with ice, and determine in a minute whether they will proceed.'

The Connemara Pony

Another pony of sound constitution, capable of living out throughout the year with only hay and windbreaks, is the Connemara. It originates in the west of Ireland, where many shopkeepers and householders in small towns like Clifden keep a pony on the mountains. Those mountains of the Irish west have to be seen to be believed. Rock covers a greater proportion than grass, and there are vast acreages of flattish rocks which the ponies learn to negotiate from the day they are born.

Probably more agile than the Dales, Fell or Highland, the Connemara has a more delicate action. 'As clever as cats on their feet', is an accurate breed society description. 'They make excellent jumpers in trappy country, are splendid jumpers, and do not "hot up".'

Connemara mare and foal, with shy two-year-old hiding from the camera. These ponies are in their natural habitat of the Irish West; note the proportion of rock to soil in the background

Colours range widely, including grey, roan, light or golden dun, bright bay, cream or black. Only piebald and skewbald are barred. They offer a greater range in size than smaller breeds, English Connemaras reaching 14.2 hands, though 14 hands is the maximum allowed in Ireland. Bridal carriages were drawn by grey horses as a sign of good luck, made better still if a grey horse was passed on the way to the ceremony. Many Connemaras are grey, but few riders will feel that the fates have been unkind if they ride any colour of this free-walking breed.

For larger trekking animals the right type of Arab or Thoroughbred cross out of any of these medium or larger British ponies is likely to be suitable, but will not winter out so well.

Imported Breeds

Three imported breeds warrant consideration for pony trekking establishments. The Icelandic pony has been bred since the ninth century, originating from Scandinavian stock to which blood from the Western Isles was later added. It is small and sturdy, usually a whole colour, with grey, dun and cream being most common. Breeding has been organised under Government sponsorship for some years, and such is the calibre of the men responsible that extremely useful types have been evolved. A draft type was formerly encouraged, but since the tractor's advent the emphasis has been on the saddle.

On many farms the ponies winter outside, living solely on what they pick up and on hay left by housed sheep. Icelandic farmers will sit up all night talking pony breeding, while their wives stay up too – to make the coffee! A great advantage of this hardy breed is the length of time allowed for maturity. The pony may run wild till it is five years old, by which time its spine is properly formed, and it then lasts well into its teens and beyond. Homing instinct is particularly strong in the Icelandic pony, as is the propensity to pace. (See Chapter 6.)

Norwegian ponies, cream in colour with stiff manes and dorsal stripe, are used at a few centres. They also are true mountain ponies, and trekking holidays can be arranged in Norway.

A more recent entrant to Britain is the Haflinger. In its home district of the Austrian Tyrol stallions have been registered for nearly a century, with government-backed breeding for 50 years. Unmistakable in colour, the Haflinger is always chestnut with dazzling flaxen mane. It looks and is a weight carrier, and is also a good horse between shafts. Quiet temperament is a carefully guarded breed characteristic.

The Haflinger Society of Great Britain claims that its protégé is the ideal mount for beginners. Hardiness is another factor, for this is a true mountain breed. In 1976 the Society's register included 320 names, mostly young stock. There are ten registered stallions, with more to be inspected. A lady trek owner in Kircudbrightshire has used Haflingers for some years, while others are found in Northumberland and Wales.

Height is 12.3 to 14.2 hands, the taller horses being encouraged.

Uniform appearance is easier to gain in a breed confined to one colour, so matching pairs or fours for driving are readily obtainable. Princess Anne has driven a Haflinger team at Windsor Show.

Strength in relation to height is a breed characteristic. On small farms in the Tyrol, Haflingers may still be the only source of power for farm operations, including ploughing and leading hay and corn. In the forests their compact frame stands them in good stead. We may well see more of these flaxen-maned chestnuts on British treks.

Exmoor pony

3 Riding and Grooming

Keep your head and your heart right up;
Keep your hands and your heels right down;
Keep your legs in close to your horse's side,
And your elbows close to your own.

Here we have the basis of horsemanship condensed into four lines. Volumes have been written on the subject, but do not let that deter you. Nor should you give up the idea of trekking because you would love to learn to ride, but are nervous, or even frightened of horses. Many a competent rider began with such feelings, which are no handicap. Instructors and ponies alike prefer someone of this disposition to the know-all, 'cowboy' types.

Horses are always approached from the nearside: the pony's left. It is from this nearside that you put on halter, bridle and saddle. You always mount from the nearside. The only time that you go to the off, far or right-hand side is for grooming or picking up the pony's feet.

Catching the pony is described in the next chapter. Leading is important. Even if you are left-handed, you must still lead the pony with your right hand, and keep the arm extended if the animal tends to walk close, or it may step on your toe. The point about care in going through gates bears repetition: take all openings squarely, remembering that a horse's shoulders are vulnerable, and it needs more room than you do. There is not room for you and your horse to pass through an average doorway at the same time; one girl groom tried this with a Clydesdale and emerged with a broken collar bone.

Your instructor will show you how to put on bit and bridle, but a point of equine anatomy is valuable here. At the back of the mouth where upper and lower gums meet, the horse has no teeth. You may therefore safely insert a thumb, and if he still won't open his jaws, tickle the roof of his mouth. This is far better than trying to force the bit in by tapping on the teeth.

When riding, *keep your head up*. The body is then steadier, the back straighter, and it is much more comfortable for your pony when you

Though the scene is Tregaron, Wales has no monopoly of wet trekking weather! Waterproof clothing which covers legs and knees is recommended. An instructress (*left*) helps a novice rider into the saddle. Hoods give good protection against wind

sit steadily and look ahead, than if its rider is forever fidgeting and turning round. *Keep your heart up*; enjoy yourself, have faith in your mount even if you have little in yourself, and this will communicate itself to the pony, who will respond by stepping out with greater verve. *Keep your hands down* and still, so that you are not irritating the pony's tender mouth. By *keeping the heels down*, you sit more firmly in the saddle. The legs are vital 'aids', and pressure from them helps urge the pony in forward and turning actions. *Elbows close to your sides* means that the forearms are in straighter line when pressure on the reins is needed, and a person riding with arms sawing at right angles looks very untidy.

Riding a trekking pony is as simple as riding a bicycle, in fact simpler because the pony stands four-square, said J. Kerr Hunter. Hold the reins between your little finger and third finger, and up between your first finger and thumb. By working the wrists you can exert leverage without moving your forearms. To move forward, give slightly with the reins and press in your legs. A light tap with the heels may be needed, and a harder one if he is stubborn, but remember to do everything on as light a rein as possible, both figuratively and in practice.

To stop, say 'Whoa, Beauty!' according to name. Take a simultaneous grip on the reins, and apply gentle but firm pressure until the pony has stopped. Don't jerk or saw on the mouth. To dismount, slip *both* feet out of the stirrups first. Then lean forward with one hand on the pommel and one gripping the mane while keeping control of the reins. Take your weight on your arms, and swing your right leg backwards over the pony's back. Then slide to the ground, still holding the reins.

When going uphill, lean forward and grip with your knees. When learning on really steep slopes, you may feel safer by taking hold of the mane or neckband. Going downhill is more difficult than going up, but lean slightly back so that your weight is just behind the pony's shoulders and grip with your knees. This 'point of balance' soon comes with practice.

Take care when riding through gates. Your pony can judge its own width to a nicety, and its own height at withers as it puts its head down to get under some obstacle. It will make no allowance for *your* width: it is up to you to keep your knees clear of gateposts and fence

High jinks in Glenshea, Perthshire. This is not part of everyday trekking, though it looks spectacular. Leather headstall with bit attached is clearly seen

sides by steering clear of them. Similarly, when thrusting under a branch, see to it that you can get through without being swept from the saddle. By lying flat along the pony's neck, you can get under fairly low branches, but don't ride too close to the one in front in case a suddenly released branch whiplashes back. Some mean ponies deliberately try to rub off their rider in this fashion, and unfortunately the trait seems most common among very small ponies and donkeys, whose riders are naturally inexperienced.

Trotting is seldom done on the trek, and cantering still less. When trotting, the rider rises to the motion of the horse, except when using a Western saddle, when sitting still is all that is required. There is another gait natural to some ponies, especially the Icelandic breed, in which the offside legs move forward together, followed by the nearside pair. This gait is called the pace or amble, and is the harness horse's means of propulsion in track events. A camel also moves in this way, but the pacing pony is more comfortable!

Don't forget that if you haven't ridden for a long time, you will be extremely stiff and sore if a long ride is attempted the first day. You must break yourself in. Riding is excellent exercise, but don't overdo it to start with; half to one hour is plenty.

Neck straps are excellent for beginners. They help cut out the desire to cling onto the reins, an abominable though quite natural fault, and give confidence to the new starter. Today's youngsters have not had that familiarity with carriage and cart horses which was inescapable among children earlier this century, and to be perched high off the ground for the first time can be rather alarming. You won't hurt the pony by any amount of pressure on a properly fitted neck strap.

The art of grooming

In addition to learning to ride, the guest must learn to groom. This is not done simply to make your pony look smart; its skin is a vital organ, and will suffer if not properly cared for. In the wild, ponies receive no grooming, yet remain perfectly healthy. Nor do they wear a saddle, for it is here that most troubles occur, and grooming encourages circulation of the blood, and gets rid of sweat. Placing a saddle on congealed accumulations of sweat is a certain way to trouble.

Grooming kit should be kept in a special box or basket. Items include the *dandy brush*, specially useful on the grass-fed pony for removing heavy dirt, caked mud and dust. The *body brush* is used for removing dust and scurf from the coat, mane and tail. Clean the body brush on a *curry comb* with its serrated edges; the metal curry comb is *not* used for direct application onto the animals, though a rubber one may be. *A wisp* is made by twisting hay into a ring.

Standing on the nearside, take the dandy brush and begin at the horse's poll. Use either arm, and concentrate on the saddle region and the lower legs. Clean from time to time by drawing across the curry comb. The body brush has a different purpose. Its close-set hairs are designed to reach right through to the skin, and it must be used so that this is achieved. Brush with short circular strokes in the same direction as the coat, and clean frequently on the curry comb.

Brush the body before the head. Remove the headstall, and put the curry comb down so that one hand is free to hold and steady the head. Work carefully and quietly. The tail is done last. Do a few locks at a time, and do not use the dandy brush, as it leaves broken hairs. Where wisping is carried out, it is done with a banging action on fleshy parts of the body. Its object is to produce a shine on the coat by squeezing out oil from the skin glands, at the same time improving the blood supply.

Getting rid of the itches of the day

Signs of Trouble

The horse world has always had its share of rogues, and some of them run trekking centres (not, we believe, on the ponies of Britain Approved List). It is no light matter for a novice to complain to an extremely 'horsey' looking groom that tack or mount are not up to scratch, but Ponies of Britain will investigate any complaint. Bad tack means discomfort for the horse and possible danger to the rider. It is up to you to let the proper people know if this occurs, for they cannot be there all the time.

Your pony's coat should be glossy, its skin loose so that you can almost pick it up by the handful. If the skin is tight and coat 'staring', the pony is out of condition. It may have worms, or simply be too old, short of food, or all three. Ribs and hip bones should not protrude. There should be no 'poverty line' down the back of the quarters. The neck should be well fleshed and muscled.

If a pony nods its head downwards on walking, it is lame in a foreleg or foot, and nods as the sound one touches the ground, to save the other one. The hip on the lame side will drop if lame behind. Correctly spotting lameness in a horse was how James Herriot got his first job as a vet in the animal film *All Creatures Great and Small*. Do not ride such a pony, and if the owners make someone else ride it, inform 'Ponies of Britain' straight away. They may be able to help that horse or pony.

If the pony sinks its back or cringes when you press the saddle area with your hand, its back is tender. If girths have pieces of lint, cotton wool or rubber tubes on them, something is definitely amiss. The skin under the girth should lie smooth; make sure it is not wrinkled before mounting. With sore or tender backs and girth galls, treatment and rest are essential *immediately*.

A saddle is built around an iron frame. If stuffing is inadequate, this frame presses down on the withers in front, or on the spine behind, *when your weight is in the saddle*. Should this occur, ask for a thick saddle cloth or blanket. Such an alleviation is only temporary, and any stable with a number of improperly maintained saddles is definitely suspect. Sometimes the animal is thin, and the saddle rests on bone instead of muscle.

Trekking ponies should always be shod. Shoes should not be embedded in the hoof or, more likely, loose. A loose shoe moves when the animal walks, and its sound on a hard surface is different from a properly secured shoe. Train your ear to appreciate the difference. Note how the points of the nails protrude through the side of the hoof. They should be clinched (flattened down), for if they project damage can be caused to the opposite leg. Feet should cause less trouble in trekking country than in cities. As Mr Jorrocks put it: 'Tain't the 'opping over 'edges as 'urts 'orses 'oofs but the 'ammer, 'ammer, 'ammer, on the 'ard 'igh road'.

Understanding Your Pony

A pony is not a machine. It has its own idiosyncrasies, dislikes and friends. It responds to treatment, for good or ill. Bad ponies are usually made, not born. The first rule is to handle your pony as gently as possible, persuading rather than forcing. The novice rider tends to take things to extremes. He literally hauls on the reins when trying to stop, as though a tug of war were necessary. He lets the reins go completely slack after stopping, so that they fall to the ground and perhaps under the pony's hoofs. This can frighten a horse if it jerks its head suddenly, and bridle or rein may be broken. A firm but gentle approach at all times is the idea.

Your pony's mouth is very sensitive. Imagine having a steel bar thrust into *your* mouth: you would wish it to be done as softly as possible. Anna Sewell's *Black Beauty* knew all about it:

'Oh! if people knew what a comfort to horses a light hand is, and how it keeps a good mouth and a good temper, they surely would not chuck, and drag, and pull at the rein as they often do. Our mouths are so tender, that where they have not been spoiled or hardened with bad or ignorant treatment, they feel the slightest movement of the driver's hand, and we know in an instant what is required of us.'

Always speak to your horse when approaching saddling up, and frequently during the ride. A pat on the neck makes for better companionship than a dig in the ribs. Your aim must be to ride a happy, good-tempered pony, and this is more readily achieved through being bright and cheerful yourself. Human moods communicate themselves immediately to the higher animals, and a horse has extra-sensory perception that enables it to be aware of things hidden to the human mind, and that includes the mood of its rider. 'Learn to understand horses with a quicker sympathy, a bolder reasoning,' said Roger Pocock.

Horse Language

Pocock, who rode and worked horses in many countries, outlined their language and reactions. When a horse throws his ears to point forward and down, and makes a short sharp snort it means 'Wheugh! Look at that, now!' If he points, snorts and shies a few yards sideways, he is playing at being in a terrible fright. One ear forward, the other back, head sideways, sidling gait may be defined as behaving in an obstreperous manner.

A horse's love call is a little whinny, soft, sweet and low, its demand for food a rumbling neigh. When your platoon passes other horses a cheery neigh means 'how d'ye do!', while a loud trumpet peal of neighing at short intervals means 'Come and join us!'

The ideal stamp of pony for smaller children. These are obviously up to the weight carried, with plenty of pony in front and behind. They are not light-boned, and the placid eye expresses an equable temperament. Halter shank on the darker pony is securely knotted out of harm's way

Ears thrown back even ever so slightly express anger. Thrown back along the neck they mean fighting rage, for wild stallions fight mainly with the teeth, and the ears are less likely to be bitten when laid flat. A sudden squeal can express rage and pretended anger.

Try to understand your horse's gestures. Stamping is merely impatience, but pawing may indicate colic. If an animal also sweats and keeps looking at its flank, something is certainly wrong. Head down and tail tucked in mean misery or sickness. 'Favouring' a forefoot, or pointing it forward, is an expression of pain in that foot.

'No creature on earth expresses feeling with sweeter quickness than a happy horse,' said Pocock. Watch the play of the nostrils. They are making a thousand comments on air-borne scents, for the horse has great powers of scent. It can smell clean standing water almost 5 miles away on a still day. The ears are constantly changing and quivering. A teamster on a four in hand or still bigger team learns to read his charges' reactions to his commands through the set of their ears, and you can do the same on your pony.

Pocock thought that the horse's scenting powers are ten times as strong as man's. He knew no horse that could see anything much more than 200 yards away. The average horse may not be able to hear at a greater distance than we can, but without doubt its sense of hearing catches vibrations above the register of human ears, and others at too close range to impress our senses.

Horses have a sense of humour. Some have been known to take off the groom's cap with their teeth and drop it in a bucket of water. They talk among themselves with a sort of thought transference, which we do not understand and cannot fully receive. The barriers between us are great, and the smell of man is probably off-putting to the fastidious creature, yet kindness goes far to breaking down these barriers. Friday night tears when guests say goodbye to their ponies prove that they have certainly vanished on one side!

Clothes for Trekking

The use of a *riding hat* is debatable. Some centres provide a selection, but a hat must fit properly, otherwise it is worse than useless. Hugh MacGregor of Aberfoyle is unequivocal: 'I have heard this point argued often. A procedure for trekking was set up that was not copied from anything, and it is one of the most natural forms of riding that can be had today. Natural riding requires *no* hard hat. I speak from 22 years of experience and I was the biggest single operator of trekking centres in Britain. In all that time very few people came with hard hats, and often they discarded them after a day or two. I have often noticed them being carried in the hand until mounting, and they are the first thing discarded on coming out of the saddle. Therefore they must be uncomfortable. There is a need for them when people do a lot of daft things such as jumping awkward jumps that a horse would not attempt if left to himself.'

A *headscarf* or sou'wester giving protection to the ears in a cold wind is an optional extra. Temperature at the top of a hill may be several degrees colder than in a snug stable yard tucked into the valley, and wind much fiercer, so be prepared. Wool, wool mixture or cotton is best for headscarves; silk or nylon tends to slip.

Warmth and comfort rather than smartness are the essentials to bear in mind when choosing clothes for trekking. Conventional riding clothes are expensive. Jodhpurs are uncomfortable when dismounted, unsuited to muddy and wet conditions and difficult to dry. Riding trousers, strong cavalry twill or corduroy are useful, particularly with a strap underfoot. Knee breeches as used by walkers are all right, as are plus-fours worn with stockings. Shorts are bad. They may be much too cold for the hills, and lead to pinching and chafing.

Today there is a large selection of windcheaters, sweaters and anoraks worn over a shirt and vest. Many of these light, warm jackets are waterproof, but they give no protection to the knees and legs. These parts suffer most discomfort in wet, so carry waterproof trousers. Waterproof coats are needed unless the weather really is fair. PVC is good, being really waterproof. You must avoid flappy material liable to scare ponies. Sailing jackets, and nylons with hood, fastening round the middle, are acceptable. Never carry glass bottles, or 'coke' in tins. Frothy drinks open with a real whoosh after a ride, and have frightened ponies.

For footwear, a good walking shoe is satisfactory. Jodhpur boots will suffice, if comfortable to walk in. Rubber riding boots tend to become too hot in summer, when most trekking is done. They also need care in drying them out overnight. Even worse to dry out are long butcher or polo boots, which are difficult to walk in and not easy to pull on or off. Such details can mar a holiday. Rubber wellingtons are unsuitable (though handy while catching the pony), while plimsolls, flat sandals and casual shoes are dangerous.

4 Daily Routine

Most treks are on a half-daily, daily or weekly basis, though some people book for a second week. Usual arrival day for weekly treks is Saturday. On Sunday morning there may be a short trek, but this is really the 'breaking in' day (for humans, not horses!). It is a great advantage if proper instruction is given at the centre, for to sit on a horse or pony can be a very alarming experience for someone quite unused to animals, as is so often the case among today's city children. In addition to elementary riding lessons, trekkers are taught the purpose of different pieces of tack and equipment, and how to use them. Grooming is discussed, demonstrated and practised. The correct way to saddle up is shown, and bridles put on. Girls who had spent three years at a London riding stables came to one trekking centre without ever having put on a bridle; someone else had always done it for them, to save time. The essence of a trekking holiday is *not* to save time; it is to learn about horses and their management, and to see as much of the countryside as possible from the saddle.

The first full day arrives. The horses are caught and brought in between 7 am and 8 am, after which the guests breakfast. Tacking up is done from 9 am to 10.30; all tack is checked, as are the ponies' feet. If shoes are loose or missing, they must be put right.

Young guests often delight in catching their own ponies, leading them in, and saddling them. At some centres this is encouraged, but it has its dangers. One of a crowd of ponies in a field corner may let fly in fun, so an instructor must supervise catching.

When catching, it is far better to carry a pocketful of nuts than a bucket of corn. The pony may refuse to pull its head out of the bucket to allow the bridle or halter to be put on. Other ponies not similarly favoured put their ears back, and may bite or lash out in jealousy. One small pony developed the habit of forcing its bucket to the ground and then turning its back to its would-be groom. If nuts are offered, the other ponies are much more likely to accept their turn patiently. When catching, put the halter shank (rope) round the pony's neck, which gives a certain hold before slipping the halter

Sunday morning scene. Early lessons from Hugh MacGregor. Note the wide range of ages, and the practical nature of the demonstration

over the face. When walking among horses it is an excellent plan *always* to carry a few titbits, whether they are being caught or not. The proper type of knot for tying up a horse will be taught. It should always be of the quick-release variety, which comes undone when the loose end is pulled. Otherwise a pony may get down in its stall, or become fast in some other place, and will hang if it cannot be quickly released.

When the ponies in a group put their ears back – saying 'I don't have to go again, do I? – something is wrong with management. In a well-run establishment, ponies don't frown. They are happy, and little feeds on going out, at midday and on return encourage the happy spirit.

Riding school methods of mounting are not necessarily best for learners. An old-fashioned mounting block is very handy. The rider can swing a leg right over the horse's back without touching it. Beginners are taught to pop up with a spring, and *not* to drag themselves up. Failing this, a 'leg up' is useful for the less fit, with the same object in view. This is *not* done with the object of saving teenage energies, but of preventing the saddle and girth from being pulled, and consequently rubbing the animal's skin. Remember at all times that prevention of saddle sores and girth galls is far, far better than cure.

Pony and Rider

Fitting the pony to the rider is much more than matching size and weight. Always be quite truthful when asked about your riding experience; nothing is easier to spot by an expert when you have been in the saddle five minutes anyway. The best riders should not have the best ponies. Ponies vary tremendously, and each string has its reliable favourites that will move at any pace with anyone. If the best riders have these, they will always be out in front. Give them the ponies that need that bit more handling, or the slug, which they cannot harm.

A steady rider can keep up with a good horse. Once a good one has been experienced, the rider will not want any other sort, and will often prefer to wait rather than go on a moderate performer. The order in which horses go out is very important. Some like to be 'front runners', and will continually try to push to the front if not put there originally. Others, like our friend the slug, are much more content tagging along behind. Ponies have friends. Your instructor should have noted which pal together when at pasture, and let them be in line together. A very small pony with novice rider should not walk behind a big one. The small one may be mischievous, especially if it is a gelding and the one in front a mare. It may nip or bite, leading to a flinging of heels from the one in front. If the ponies are matched for size, the offender will take a knock, and serve it right, but a big leader may lash over a small follower's head and catch the child rider. Always be on the lookout to prevent such accidents.

The first mile may be the most difficult part of the trek. Often it entails road work, and all riders should receive full instructions regarding order and speed before setting out. Reasonable distances between mounts should be maintained until open country or easier going affords a more relaxed attitude.

Changing horses during the trek is bad practice. It entails more mounting and dismounting, with riders half in and half out of the saddle doing untold damage to a tender back. Stick to your allotted pony, unless there is a very good reason for change.

This first day's trek is not long. There is usually a gentle ride till 12.30 pm, then an hour's break for lunch. A further two hours' steady riding brings the party back to stables about 3.30 pm. Each day the rides get longer and more strenuous, with Wednesday as midweek rest day at some centres. Always remember that while you are on holiday, your pony is not. It is working a five-and-a-half- or six-day week, and will do the same next week and the week after.

The midday break should be planned beforehand. Your instructor stops at the appointed place, where grazing is available. Slacken the girth, run up the stirrup irons as you have been shown. Remove the bit from the horse's mouth and allow it to water quietly. Give it plenty of time, and do not pull into a bunch of others, or allow others to come too near. Your pony drinks with confidence if not in a crush, without fear of being bumped. If you wish you may estimate how much it is drinking. Aime Tschiffely did, on his 10,000 miles trek from Buenos Aires to Washington:

'Off and on we travelled on the very shores of the lake, and many a cool drink did the horses have. Often I counted the gulps they swallowed, watching them go down their necks with the regularity of the pulse. When they had taken their fill they would open their nostrils wide and give a long snort, rather like a German when he has drained the last drop of beer out of his massive pewter; and then they often pawed the water in play, as if annoyed at not being able to drink more.'

Your instructor will say if saddles and bridles are to be removed to a safe place, setting the saddle pommel to ground. Tie up the ponies to a picket line, which is simply a rope tied taut between two fixed points, usually trees. Use the headstall and halter shank for this purpose. If there is no grazing, a nosebag feed must be carried.

Better still, use the pony trekkers' hobble. The halter shank is taken round the near foreleg in a half-hitch, instead of being lashed round the neck. It goes back through the halter ring.

A pony thus hobbled can lie down and rest, graze or roll. He can wander but he cannot gallop away. This is much better than tethering, when ponies start rubbing, getting their feet over the tether, or pulling at the fence, but the pony must be trained to its use.

As the trek progresses homewards, the ponies become aware that

Watering the ponies at Loch Ard, Aberfoyle, epitomises the peace and beauty that makes trekking such a wonderful experience. Horses watering or feeding should be given plenty of room

they are going back to their food and familiar surroundings, rather than away from them as in the morning. They thus tend to walk more freely. Most trekking will be away from busy roads, but some road work may be inevitable on leaving or returning to the centre.

Traffic Safety Rules

Traffic coming from behind poses the bigger problem. On busy roads, all riders should be tight into their side of the road the whole time. Be aware of the instructor at all times. Always be in single file where there is possibility of traffic. Some car drivers are idiots, but so are some horsemen. It is sheer bad manners to walk or trot slowly along a narrow lane where the car or lorry cannot pass you. The rider may think: 'Just look how nice I look on my horse', but the car driver is not thinking that at all. A string of 19 quiet horses is easily upset by the 20th foolish rider.

The Royal Society for the Prevention of Accidents presents a supplement to the Highway Code. The British Horse Society and the Pony Club have helped with advice.

RIDING ALONE OR IN A SMALL PARTY:

Look ahead and ride straight.

Keep well in to the left.

Ride in single file if the road is at all narrow or has bends.

Leader walk or jog at a steady pace to avoid the rear file having to trop up fast.

Look both ways before moving off, turning or halting.

If trotting, go steady round all corners.

Have your reins short enough for your horse to be really under control.

Obey police, traffic control signals and traffic lights.

Give way to pedestrians at zebra crossings.

Look behind and in front before you pull out to pass a stationary vehicle, to make sure the road is clear.

It is *not* your road when a vehicle is stationary in front of you on your side of the road, ie when a vehicle or person coming towards you has the right of way.

Ride on the grass verge where possible (some local councils forbid it).

In a built-up area be considerate for mown grass in front of houses and elsewhere.

If your horse shies, turn his head away from the object and *don't look at it yourself.*

You need not ride in silence *but* keep alert to road conditions.

LEADING

If leading another horse when mounted, have it on your nearside and conform with other road users by riding on the left side of the road. When leading on foot, always place yourself between your horse and the traffic but, on a road without a footpath, walk on the right-hand side of the road and keep your horse close to the edge.

Be careful when passing pedestrians, particularly so if your horse is difficult.

Pat your horse and speak to him if he is nervous of high vehicles.

Look ahead and walk straight.

CROSSING A MAIN ROAD OR AT A JUNCTION

If in a party, never start to cross a road until all the riders are near enough to cross together. Wait until the road is clear enough to allow the whole party to cross in safety.

Never get separated – some on one side of the road and some on the other. Take special care on the road in twilight or in fog and mist.

RIDING OR LEADING ON A SLIPPERY ROAD

Get off it as soon as possible.

Trust your horse and let him walk on.

He does not want to fall. If you leave him alone he is less likely to slip.

On icy roads quit your stirrups.

If your horse falls, pick yourself up and let him get up. Pat him.

Do not try to mount where it is still slippery.

If leading, do not try to pull your horse along.

Hold the reins lightly so that you can let go if your horse falls, and walk on. He will follow.

Concentrate on keeping your own feet.

SNOW

Stop at a garage or farm. Ask for *thick* motor grease.

Smear thickly on soles and frogs on all four feet.

The snow will then not ball. If going far do this more than once.

BE COURTEOUS

Be considerate and help others on the road.

Acknowledge the courtesy of other road users with a gesture.

Pass others at a walk on a bridle path or narrow road.

Three words to remember –

Alertness; Anticipation; Courtesy

Pony first, you second

On returning from the trek, the routine is to stall up, strip and feed the ponies. Then comes perhaps the most enjoyable meal of the day for guests: afternoon tea, with hot drinks, scones, jam and cakes. Never does it taste so good as after a long spell in the saddle, with appetite whetted and the prospects of an evening's relaxation ahead.

But not yet. After tea the stalls must be cleaned out and the yard swept. This half-hour break is invaluable to the ponies, as it gives time for any swellings to appear. Each pony must be carefully looked over,

Mucking-out and sweeping the yard prove enjoyable to this party of trekkers. Such jobs are part of horse management, and cleaning, feeding and grooming invoke as much pleasure as the actual riding in keen horsemen and women

especially for lameness or any sign of saddle sores or girth galls. Dried sweat is brushed off, or washed off at some centres. Putting a saddle on caked sweat does untold damage. On turning out, the pony may immediately roll, and apparently undo all the care lavished on him, but this is not so. Though his hide may gather a few leaves or bits of grass, fundamentally it is in good condition for the next day's trek.

The corn or horse nut feed is known as 'concentrate', which describes it exactly. It has high nutrient value in small bulk, and the horse's stomach appreciates this, and so it feels satisfied and content to rest for a while before indulging in serious grazing.

Backs should be washed off in the yard, if done as an aid to preventing sore backs and shoulders. Your instructor will show you how to do it, but it is essentially a cold douche, well brushed in, over the saddle area. Tack is cleaned under supervision once a week.

Remember that the pony is yours for the week. Its health and comfort depend on the way you become a horseman by implicitly following the simple rules outlined.

Horses should always be walked for the last mile. If they canter or trot they will arrive in a sweat, and take longer to cool off. When ready to turn into the paddock for the night, lead your charge by its head collar or halter shank, pass through the gate with ample clearance on either side, walk into the field a little way and swing the horse round towards you, ie facing the gate. Then slip off the headstall, and do not flick it over the rump as a goodnight gesture, or it may not be so easy to catch again. A spirited horse may swing round on gaining its freedom, and lash out its heels from *joie de vivre*, not malice. If you are within range the effect is the same, however, and by facing the horse towards you, the kick is more likely to miss than if you allow it to dash past on its way to pasture.

People inured to city routine tend to become upset if the ride does not end at the scheduled time, say 4.30 pm. The Dutch and Germans, who work punctiliously to a timetable at home, are especially prone to this inability to relax. What does it matter? You are governed only by the needs of your horse and breakfast and evening meal bells, the last two of which you are extremely unlikely to miss! For the rest, adjust your timing to that of the countryside about you, and forget about clocks. Overseas guests sometimes take a week before they relax properly.

After dinner comes relaxation. If you want bingo, stay in Blackpool or Brighton, not on a farm tucked under the Welsh hills or the Scottish mountains. Children should have no difficulties at all in amusing themselves at a trekking centre, for usually there are animals to play with, and sometimes interesting and rare breeds of stock are kept for visitors' delight. There is usually a stream nearby, fish to catch, or wild fruit to gather, but early bed is the best rule when trekking. When you have had 15 or 20 miles in the saddle, the last thing you will need is a sleeping pill.

5 Where to Trek

Among pony trekking's chief joys is its surprising way of leading to unexpected holes and corners and delightful scenery. Britain is referred to as 'this tiny island', but whoever coined the phrase probably never left London! It is perfectly possible to get lost in a great many districts, for trekking is, fortunately, concentrated in the wilder and more inaccessible regions of our islands. The wide south-west moors, the open spaces of the New Forest, the green hills and woods of Wales, austere Pennine and abrupt Lakeland scenery contrast with rides by Scottish lochs, and climbs within sight of its highest mountains.

The West Country

Dartmoor is a favourite. Lying on the western half of Devon, it stretches for over 20 miles from Okehampton in the north to Ivybridge in the south, and is almost 20 miles from east to west. Haytor and Mary Tavy mark these east/west boundaries, and what lovely names have been given to Devon villages! Yelverton, Sticklepath and Haytor belong unmistakably to the south-west, just as Mossthwaite could only be in the northern hills.

Though the open moor is unfenced, it is abutted by enclosures and hewtakes. Some of these are open to the public for riding, and some are not. Ask locally. On the open moor, there is no restriction in law; nature provides her own. The worst bogs are on the highest ground, as they are on many British hills, and boulders make riding impracticable in some parts.

In others, rocks and rough ground are such that the territory may be crossed at a walk. There are three main rules when riding on Dartmoor; break any of them and you could be in trouble. The first is *never* to attempt to ride across the centre of the moor. If you are in sight of enclosed land you are generally all right, for the region of really bad bogs has not been reached. The second rule concerns bogs which lie close to streams and rivers. Avoid flowing water unless there is a definite track or ford; stick to the higher ground and look down onto it. The third rule applies to most parts of the country. Make local enquiries about the rides in the districts. Do not plan long rides on Dartmoor without a guide.

We have all heard of the grim fogs that descend on Dartmoor, and though they are less likely in spring and summer, riders should be on their guard. Here again, local advice is invaluable. Your trek leader is unlikely to be caught, and will know what to do if a fog descends rapidly. Should you be out alone or with a small party unfamiliar with the moor, trust your ponies. If fogs surround you and show no sign of lifting, the only thing to do is to let the reins go slack and rely on your mounts' instincts. Many a hill farmer has been lost in a fog on his own land, and returned home through his pony's sense of direction. To be lost in fog can be a frightening experience, and one that should not arise, but be prepared.

We leave the dreary fogs and return to Churchill's vision of 'broad, sunlit uplands'. This makes an ideal description of Dartmoor on a fine day, for it has miles and miles of springy turf, and acres of heather, which you and your pony will love. You may ride far and long without crossing a road, or even encountering the farmed valleys which run up onto the moor.

Dartmoor is real horse country, and there is wide choice of trekking centres. If you wish to see as much of Dartmoor's expanse as possible, stay a few days at one centre, then move to another. To ride each day to a different centre is not advisable. It would entail more road work, and some villages are not easy to approach from the moor without a guide. Principal holiday towns and villages near good riding country are Okehampton, Belstone, Sticklepath, Chagford, Moretonhampstead, Lustleigh and Haytor to the north and east of Dartmoor. To the south and west are Ashburton, Buckfastleigh, Brent, Ivybridge, Yelverton, Horrabridge, Tavistock, Mary Tavy, Lydford and Bridestowe, while Widecombe and Hexworthy lie in the middle.

Cornwall is well-equipped with riding centres. To ride in its soft airs over moor, through forest and down its innumerable country lanes is a delightful experience. Some centres include overnight camping in their schedule. Bodmin Moor has tremendous views, and gives excellent riding for competent parties under an experienced guide, and views of the Atlantic rollers are seldom far away.

Riding in Somerset has many advantages. Distances from the main residential towns are less, and wild open country is combined with woodland rides. Exmoor has its own breed of pony, and you may well be lucky and see these while trekking across the moor (See Chapter 2).

The former counties of Herefordshire and Worcestershire offer delightful riding country. Herefordshire has the second lowest population density in the United Kingdom, a mild climate, and varied if not really wild scenery. It has a good deal of grassland as befits the home of a world-famous breed of cattle. William Cobbett wrote in his famous early nineteenth-century *Rural Rides*:

'The country is very fine all the way from Ross to Hereford. The soil is always a red loam upon a bed of stone. The trees are very fine, and certainly winter comes later here than in Middlesex. Some of the oak trees are still perfectly green (November 10) and many of the ashes as green as in September.'

Warwickshire is another county with some splendid grassland, while Wiltshire and Hampshire offer fine upland riding. Here the countryside is mostly arable, and green roads through waving seas of corn hold the eye.

Journeying from south-east Hampshire to London, Cobbet wrote: 'The air upon the South Downs is saltish, I dare say; and the clouds may bring something a little partaking of the nature of sea water'.

The New Forest

Most of England's southern and eastern counties sport at least one centre. The best known unenclosed area in the south is the New Forest, with over 100 square miles of land in public ownership, and a further 40 in all. Provided no damage is done to woodland or game, and no fires are lit or litter left, the New Forest is open to general access. It is well watered, and criss-crossed by innumerable sandy tracks which are ideal for novices and other riders.

Organisation is good. There are a number of village centres, but farms in the usual sense do not exist. They are smallholdings with little land, and little accommodation. Brockenhurst, Burley, Stoney Cross and Norley Wood all offer places to stay. The New Forest Hunts Branch of the Pony Club covers the entire Forest.

This branch and local riding schools will help in piloting strangers around the area's bogs. These are dangerous, for although they are not difficult to spot once you have learned what to look for, and ponies can identify them, they are a distinct hazard to the unaccustomed eye. Flies are a New Forest snag, the only relief to man and beast being a fly-switch and the wearing of ear caps. Adders are also common, but will rarely bite a pony. Should either horse or rider be bitten, the main rule is to rest and avoid all strain on the heart. 'Springs' of liquid clay going deep into the ground are marked by regulars with a long stick, so keep clear of such signs or your pony may disappear down to its belly. If lost, rely on your pony, or follow the first gravelled road, which will join others. There is more chance of being able to use the sun as compass than in most parts of Britain.

Trekking in Wales

A horseman feels at home in Wales. During the journey to any centre of your choice, ponies by the score will be seen from car or train. There is no escaping them in the Principality. Nowhere is this more apparent than in Brecon, under those towering Beacons which have caused trouble to many a walker. They are high, far higher than they look because of their smooth grassy surface and absence of surrounding deep valleys to give contrast and warning. The tops of the Beacons are little lower than the summit of Snowdon, yet of completely different character. They can be very cold. Hence the trekker in those parts must be specially well prepared, and heed local advice. Rainfall can be heavy here, as in most hill districts, but when the sun comes out the contrasting shadows ornament a marvellous countryside.

The Black Mountains offer much choice. They are yet another area giving full scope to the rider who wishes to get well away from town life. No district of south Wales is better than another in this respect, and there will be ample choice of pony. Large herds breed on the mountains, and only the best are retained for home use. Probably no breed except Welsh will be ridden, but they offer a complete range (See Chapter 2). Welsh people are intensely and rightly proud of their native livestock, and if you are within distance of the Royal Welsh Show at Builth Wells, in late July, try to visit. Welsh ponies and cobs are at their best and there is even a pony trekking class.

The Lake District

For scenery, the Lake District and the Pennines are hard to beat. Lakeland was concerned with the tourist trade long before most other rural areas, and has held onto its lead. Accommodation can always be arranged, and there is no shortage of interesting rides. The combination of water and mountain for which the district is world famous is best seen from the saddle; sound paths under a scree face alternate with detours round swamps and long walks over sound, springy turf. Ponies are likely to be mixed; the Fell is native to the area, but smaller ponies are imported. One centre specialises in Icelandic ponies, which find the mild Lakeland climate to their liking.

Though rainfall can be heavy, all centres are well equipped against it. If rain falls in Lakeland, you do not wait till it clears, but tog up and meet the elements. Then the return and the hot meal have an added flavour. Do not be put off by the fact that Lakeland foxhunting is on foot, not horseback. Hounds must follow the fox whichever way he chooses to run, and many of those rocky chasms are quite inaccessible on horseback. For a cross country trek, however, there are many suitable paths and bridleways, and it is possible to follow those which are away from the main walkers' routes.

Congestion is a Lakeland problem. It is confined to the roads and a few towns, for even at peak weekends there are lots of parts to visit where only a handful of people are seen. The Lake District covers 600 square miles, which is a lot of room, and unlike pony trekkers, many visitors can only be happy where entertainment is laid on for them.

The Pennines

Though the rest of northern England is not as well known to the tourist, it is well served with trekking centres. The Derbyshire High Peak District has its own charm, and rides within the Peaks National Park are possible. Always remember that the sign 'National Park' does not give licence to roam anywhere; you are still on private property and all the land has its particular purpose, just as elsewhere.

Some centres lie near Yorkshire and Lancashire industrial areas, for boundary between town and open spaces is sharply divided on the Pennines. There are few sprawling suburbs, but mills and factories one minute, the brown-green hills, curlew and grazing sheep the next. Further north are centres near Hawes on the Pennine Way,

Early trekkers. All the wool once manufactured at Kendal, Cumbria, was transported by pack ponies, forerunners of the modern Fell. In a 1975 Tableau, at Lowther, Cumbria, Fells re-enacted the scene, also taking part in spectacular displays by Border reivers, who rode this sturdy pony

while another trek crosses Pendle Hill, home of the Lancashire witches.

Fine riding country is to be found on the North York Moors. It is hunted regularly by mounted packs – the Bilsdale, Farndale, Staintondale, Saltersgate and Goathland – and has many private stables, but few horses for hire. Miles of heather are interspersed with green valleys, green roads and tracks.

Crossing to the western Pennines we come to a district known locally as East Fell Side. When riding on these slopes the rider looks westwards to the Cumbrian Mountains – the Lakeland hills – and so has a double choice. The high Pennine country with its moorland looking down onto rich mixed farming is to hand, while only a few miles away Lakeland riding begins. There are some extremely wide open spaces of little-known riding country above East Fell Side.

On this west side the Scottish border is quickly reached, but on the east Northumberland tapers northwards for many miles. That is a great riding county, with splendid Thoroughbred horses, and studs of most pony breeds. There are centres near Hexham, close to the Roman Wall, and Belford, near the sweeping bays of Northumbria's coastline. The county is sparsely populated away from Newcastle and adjoining industrial and mining areas, hence accommodation is not easy to find. Farms are large, and not generally dependent on tourism, but anyone with an interest in horses will find a warm welcome.

Around Cheviot is some of Britain's wildest country, easing to fertile mixed farming before the Lammermuirs are reached. These hills under an August and September sun are a mass of brilliant purple, and Gifford is a useful centre. Grouse figure highly in the Scottish moors' economy, so always find where and when to ride.

Scottish Border Country

The Borders are great riding country. They have a horse atmosphere, enhanced at such events as Riding the Bounds at Langholm and Peebles. Galloway, once known for its own breed of pony, now regrettably extinct, is off the main tourist route to the Highlands, and worthy of a separate holiday. It has some good trekking, and Norwegian ponies are kept at one centre. Ayrshire has splendid scenery away from the industrial areas, which are soon left way behind, while northwards is the large county of Argyll. This has pleasant if at times rather wet climate. Grazing is surprisingly good even on the highest mountains; your ponies will eat clover growing at 2,000ft, and shelter from the wind can always be found.

The Highland pony now figures more and more on the lists. There is always a special pleasure in riding a native, and Highland ponies will be seen on crofts and farms, as far as Sutherland and Caithness. Though there are centres at Ullapool, they are more common on the east of Scotland. From Stirling, Perth and Moray to Aberdeen and Inverness, trekking is well organised and popular. The countryside offers rich variety, and any illusions that all the best land in Britain is in the south are quickly shattered among the raspberry plantations of Angus and Abberdeen. It is real stockman's country, where horse enthusiasts are welcome.

Perthshire includes some of Britain's finest trekking country, as befits a county that established Britain's second centre. Aberfoyle is one convenient centre within reach of the Trossachs and the wild country surrounding Lock Art – the country of Rob Roy. Though not really high, and so less likely to be cold, these hills have grand views of the Wallace Monument, Stirling Castle and Ben Lomond.

Fresh treks for every day of the week are planned from Aberfoyle. Woodland riding is interspersed with treks on the open tops, and co-operation from both local farmers and the Forestry Commission is excellent. One farmer said to the operator: 'Tell me where you want a gate in our new fence line, and I'll put one in'.

This is the sort of attitude that makes trekking possible, and in Scotland, the land of a million views, there is ample room for responsible trekkers.

Good trekking is to be had in Ross-shire, and here you really are among the wide open spaces. Island riding has its own fascination.

Arran and Mull possess their full share of fine rides, and as on all the Western islands there is a surprising amount of open country. Residents are often strict Sabbatarians, so there may well be no Sunday riding.

Ireland

Cross the Irish sea and you are once more in horseman's country. Trekking centres near Dublin contrast with stables near the rocky west coast, and if your trip coincides with the Dublin horse show and

Water in the background as this trek leaves Loch Lubnaig. A far greater variety of mountain and loch may be seen from the saddle than from one's own two feet

sales, that is an event not to be missed. Naturally, Connemara ponies predominate in Ireland (See Chapter 2). In addition to the delights of riding these fine ponies over such varied country, there is the lure of sea and river fishing and golf, with shooting and hunting in winter. Look out for that interesting breed the Irish Draft, a large, well-made horse which may not be available to trekkers, but your guide will know of it.

One big advantage of Irish trekking is absence of heavy traffic. Even if you go on roads, there is little to worry about, except perhaps the effect on your mount of donkeys hauling milk churns! In Galway you are in Somerville and Ross country, and there is no better way of spending an evening after riding than reading of the exploits of Flurry Knox, Smiler and the redoubtable Major Yeates in the days when the horse was undisputed king. The Major described the Irish west as:

'It was a perfect morning in August. She and I were seated in incredible leisure, on a space of sward that sank in pleasant curves to the verge of the summer sea. We looked across three miles of burnished water to the Castle Manus hills that showed mistily through grey veils of heat.'

Or, as evocative:

'The weather next morning was a welter of wind and mist, with rain flung in at intervals. The golden fox on the stable weathercock was not at peace for a moment, facing all the southern points of the compass as if they were hounds that held it at bay. . . . I trotted on through the rain, up a steep road seamed with watercourses, with Lonen Hill towering on my left, and a lesser hill on my right. We laboured upwards, parallel with the covert, while the wind, heavy with mist, came down to meet us, and shoved against us like a living thing.'

Country people are much the same the world over and Icelanders equal the British in love of horses. Their sturdy ponies usually live on the mountains, so are well able to conduct you over those regions of clear air, immensely long summer days and brown or white sheep. Further afield, Spain, Hungary and the USA offer trekking holidays, for no more positive way of seeing another country exists.

Amenities Round the Country
A trekking holiday suits families or individuals. A quick tour of Britain shows the variety of facilities available. A Cambridgeshire farm caters mainly for children, who sleep in an annexe to the farmhouse, and have large playroom, books and table tennis as well as a cross country course. Cornwall has a farm taking young people from 12 to 25 and self catering family parties; surfing and riding are both available. In Lakeland one trekking centre guarantees qualified staff, guests staying at nearby hotels. Instruction in stable management is given in Derbyshire, with guests living as family, but also two

caravan sites offering no facilities except piped water. This contrasts with a Gloucestershire establishment with heated swimming pool, badminton and TV.

Smoking is banned at one Devon centre, with Western trail riding around Exmoor in May, June and September. At a Dorset stables, gymkhanas, shows, horse fairs and beaches are offered. No road work is involved at a Hampshire riding school adjoining the New Forest; it has nearby hotels, guest houses, camping and caravan sites. If Leicestershire is your choice, a non-residential riding school has accommodation in a neighbouring farmhouse, and takes unaccompanied children from nine upwards. No beginners or novices are taken at an Oxfordshire centre, but there are special rates for school parties, and guests can be collected from London Airport or a nearby station. There is also a diploma preparation course.

Children of parents living abroad are specially catered for on a Somerset farm, where a modernised Georgian farmhouse is available. Families and children with their own ponies are also welcomed. In Surrey there is a riding centre for the handicapped, with fees of up to 50p per half hour paid for either by parents or administrative authorities. In Sussex unaccompanied children of 8–15 live under canvas, with farmhouse accommodation during term time, complete with record player, tennis court, central heating, colour TV and swimming.

A West Yorkshire riding school takes two residents only. Instruction is given on reliable horses at all stages from beginner to advanced rider. By contrast, one Argyllshire centre caters purely for the casual holiday rider, with morning, afternoon and evening rides of two hours' duration. In East Lothian, 'home from home' accommodation is offered, overlooking the sea. Youth hostel camping site is nearby with transport arranged to the centre, and while toilets are provided, trekkers bring their own sleeping bags. Exmoor ponies are used here, with anyone over 12 stone mounted on a Highland pony.

If you wish to trek in the Great Glen, Inverness-shire, chalets sleeping up to six may be rented, with hill, moorland, and riverside riding, youngsters under ten being accompanied on the leading rein. In Kirkcudbright, hotel guests use Highland ponies, and have a Festival Theatre, cinema and golf course on their doorstep. Touring caravans and tents are welcome in Wigtonshire, with a 'take away' shop, launderette, shop, play area and TV lounge. Fishing, putting, sailing, water skiing and rowing are available in addition to trekking over quiet countryside at hourly rates. In Wales, a Caernarvonshire stud offers trekking on Welsh cobs, fishing and a bowling green. In Carmarthen, non-riding guests live in caravans, with cottage and ranch-type accommodation for school parties and unaccompanied children. Riders take their pony for a week, and have complete charge of it under strict supervision.

Salmon and trout fishing, shooting and two golf courses are alternative attractions near Llangollen, with separate rides for experienced and novice riders. Home cooking using game and Welsh produce is a speciality here. Driving weeks are offered during off-peak periods at Abergavenny, with free camping field for Guides and Scouts.

In Radnorshire, resident dogs are welcomed at one hotel, but most trekking is for students and young people of 14–25.

6 What to See

Wildlife is not afraid of horses. This simple fact explains the advantage of the mounted observer over *all* other methods of nature study. As the line of ponies jingles along the hillside, fox, cuckoo, stonechat or weasel remain customarily wary, as they must throughout every waking moment, but they do not instantly take flight as they would from the sound and scent of a man on foot.

The rider is perched higher than the walker; a 10-year-old girl may scarcely be able to see over the stone walls from her own two feet, but seated on even quite a small Welsh or Icelandic pony she can view the surrounding countryside from her mobile vantage point to considerable benefit. She can look above the thorn hedge at the blackbird nesting by the wood corner, noting the duller female plumes and the cock's bright yellow bill without having to watch her own step; the pony does that for her. The sunken lanes of Cornwall or Wales present a barrier to distant views on foot, but to the mounted platoon come glimpses of field or sea. Untrammelled by vast packs, the horseman is free to hold up his head and look around him. His essential belongings are tucked neatly into saddlebags, not towering above him in a swaying nylon cover!

Though a great deal of country may be seen on a walking holiday, the horse multiplies the amount. A trek of 20 miles a day is not arduous, whereas a walk of that distance tries to the limit anyone out of training. This advantage of sheer distance vastly enhances the value of trekking to the watcher of nature. Many of Britain's wildest parts, most interesting for the naturalist, are several miles from the nearest village, and to walk there is very time consuming and cuts down the chance to wait and observe.

A word of warning is necessary regarding use of binoculars on horseback. Do not constantly flash them about. They are no part of the quietest pony's normal routine, and it is especially upsetting to sling them loosely on the back, flapping about and putting your mount on edge. A small pair packed in the saddlebag is permissible, but it is best to use them for something really unusual and distant.

Gipsy pony

Everything in the countryside is done for a purpose. If you wish to discover different parts of Britain, there is no better way than by holidaying at a succession of centres in different localities. Even the gates, stone walls and hedges are different. The Yorkshire dales are famous for their stone walls and the stone barns formerly used to store hay for the winter. Stone there is very suitable for walling, whereas in parts of the south west the walls are surmounted by a hedge to temper fierce winds fresh from the Atlantic. Even the stiles through or over the walls vary between districts.

Gates and gate fasteners also vary. They are of practical importance to the horseman, and in an ideal world would all swing freely, and close easily. Unfortunately there are a lot of 'shoulder gates' around, which necessitate physical lifting from ground level to open and shut them. Some trekking centres set new gates as a gesture of goodwill towards the farmer who allows them over his land, even though he cannot legally stop them. 'Give and take' is a prime if unspoken countryside rule, and you never know when some emergency will occur when the only shelter is a nearby farmhouse.

A popular gate fastener is the swinging rail, which should fasten itself when the gate swings to. Setting gate posts and swinging the

No need for a famous bridge to cross the Forth at this point. Trekkers from Aberfoyle do so regularly, and use of fords like these add a spice of adventure to the holiday. The last pony takes its chance to drink

gate on its hinges is another of those apparently simple operations which in reality demands skill and practice. Do not undo this work by rough handling. The hook-and-eye is another type of fastener, or the gate may be fitted with a flat piece of sprung steel easily pulled back by hand. All variations are worth recording in the holiday log book.

Hedges and walls

The age of a hedge may be assessed by the number of kinds of tree or bush in it. One for every hundred years of life is a rough guide, and hedges primarily of hawthorn or blackthorn may also contain holly, hazel, ash and other hardwoods. Note the shelter afforded by a good hedge when you reach its lee side on a breezy day; many a countryman before you has been similarly grateful.

Wildlife is often to be seen in hedgerows or on walls. The sight of a weasel or stoat hunting along a dry stone wall, endlessly easing its lithe body in and out of the spaces, has been watched for an amazing duration from the saddle. Pheasants too run along a hedge, and rabbits make tracks through; the padded path soon becomes distinguishable to the practised eye. Sunken wells with a pivoting lid are sometimes incorporated where rabbits pass through a stone wall; the rabbits jump on top and then down into the smooth-sided trap.

The best stone walls are double-faced. They start on a firm foundation, the two 'cheeks' of the wall being made independently, and the space between filled with small rubble. Note the lines of 'throughs' – large flat stones which protrude on either side of the wall and bind the whole together. As the wall narrows near the top, it becomes only one stone wide, surmounted by a row of coping stones set on edge. Hundreds of miles of these walls have been built throughout Britain without an ounce of cement, and it is an art at which the British, and their kin in the former Dominions, excel. Fortunately it is not a dying craft. County councils have built many miles of new stone walls, and employed skilled countrymen to do so. During breaks, do not scramble over the walls, or you will surely dislodge stones. Use the nearest gate or stile.

Farm stock often congregates under a wall or hedge, especially on a windy day. Note as many different breeds as you can. Besides our native breeds of cattle and sheep there are numerous crosses between

Last through close the gate. Always open gates to their full width, to avoid scraped knees. The instructor is shutting the gate in this case, and is well enough mounted to ride up and down the line to ensure that everyone is happy. Keep in line when asked, to avoid spreading hoof damage over pasture

them, with the picture further complicated by foreign imports. Yet there are a few simple starting points.

Spotting Cattle Breeds

Cattle with white faces have a Hereford as sire, except in the case of Simmental crosses, where the beasts usually have brown 'spectacles' round their eyes. The pure Hereford may be found in its native county and parts of Wales and the Midlands. Its rich-red body colour contrasts with white head and white stripe along the spine. The Hereford has starred in a hundred Western films, where other riders have sought to capture it with the lasso.

More common in northern England and Scotland are the Aberdeen Angus and the Galloway. Both are black and polled (hornless). Both sprang from the same roots, but the modern Angus is blockier, with fine, smooth coat, whereas the Galloway has long guard hairs and a dense, mossy undercoat as befits its struggle with the upland elements.

There are also dun Galloways, and the unmistakable Belted Galloways, with broad white belt around a black or dun body. Note how easily these are seen at a distance; the white belt shows up on a dull afternoon, and the black part in snow. The Belties were greatly loved by your predecessors on the drove roads for the same reason. They showed up at dusk, one or two being sufficient to mark a large herd.

When trekking in Wales, another black breed is certain to hove into view. The Welsh Black generally has horns, is of medium size, and has made almost as great a world-wide reputation as the Welsh pony or cob you may well be riding.

Red Devons are frequently found in the south-west, the rich ruby-red of the North Devon contrasting with the lighter shade of the enormously large South Devon. Sussex and Lincoln Reds complete the trio of red breeds, each still most popular in its native county. The Shorthorn is red, red and white or roan. Had you been trekking between the wars this is the breed you would have found over much of England. It lost ground to the Ayrshire – commonly mahogany – red and white in varying proportions – and more so to the black and white Friesian. The latter is a big cow needing plenty of food to enable it to produce its vast quantities of milk for the townsman's daily pint, and so is often found in the lower dales and plains.

Lastly, and less often found in trekking districts, are the beautiful little Jerseys and their slightly bigger fellow Channel Islanders, the Guernseys. They give rich milk and yellow cream, vary in colour from light fawn to almost black in the case of the Jerseys, and the cows are very gentle. In contrast to the docile females, Jersey bulls are very fierce, being descendants of the Spanish fighting bulls. Fortunately they are seldom found in a field, and bulls are not a likely hazard on regular trekking routes. Cows with young calves can be equally dangerous however, and on no account get between a cow and its calf, or she may rush back to it quite regardless of any obstacle in the path. This is an unlikely contingency, as newly born calves tend to lie away from the rest for a few days. A more probable encounter is with a bunch of young heifers, who come galloping and kicking up their heels in a rather alarming fashion if you are not sure what they are. All cattle are inquisitive, and these youngsters before the cares of matrimony more so than most, but they will pull up with sliding hoofs a few yards from the line of riders. Nonetheless they can cause momentary apprehension. Ride steadily on, and they will ignore you eventually.

No one needs help in recognising Highland cattle. Brown, yellow-red or brindle, they have been painted and photographed times without count in their native glens. Despite their ferocious appearance, Highlanders are quiet cattle. Even the bulls are usually gentle, though no bull, boar or stallion is really to be trusted. The Highlanders' quiet trait comes from selection during the 'shieling' days, when whole families accompanied their cattle to the high summer grazings of the short Scottish summer. It was hardly likely that a temperamental bull would be kept where children were playing. The sweep of horn is perfectly controlled by the Highlander. They can swing through a narrow gate to within a fraction of an inch, and are so accurate that they 'can flick a tick off their flanks', as one cattleman said. Notice their neat hoofs. Any of you would be proud to have a horse with such shapely feet.

Companions of the Highland cattle are Scottish Blackface sheep. Their name is not really accurate; they may have varying amounts of white on their faces, but their straight grey wool and curling horns make them unmistakable. The other Scottish hill sheep is the Cheviot, white faced, white woolled and white of leg. It may be crossed with the Border Leicester of the Roman nose and stylish carriage, that in Allan Fraser's words 'steps like a hackney horse on clean boned legs, that carries itself as though fountains at Versailles still played for a queen'.

Trekking across Welsh hills you may also find the Border Leicester, mated to the little sandy-faced Welsh Mountain ewe to produce another white breed, the Welsh Halfbred. The Black Welsh Mountain is also an interesting sheep.

One of our most endearing breeds is the little Herdwick of the Lakeland fells. The green valley fields are scattered with black lambs in May, their dams turning grey and eventually almost white with age. There are some excellent trekking centres in Lakeland, with marvellous views, and the higher your pony climbs the more likely are Herdwicks to be the dominant breed. A group of rams (breeding males) was being driven from the hirings, crossing from Keswick to Buttermere, for Herdwick rams may be hired for the season. Thick

'There is no secret so close as that between a horse and his rider', said Surtees. Trekkers in Glenshee are discovering the truth of this in an awe-inspiring background

mist fell on the mountain tops, and at unmarked crossroads the rams wanted to go one way, their hardy Lakeland owners the other. The men forced the sheep against their will, only to find themselves completely lost. They gave the animals their head, and were led back safely into the very farmyard that was their goal. You are unlikely to be lost with a guide, but if ever fog catches you alone and unawares, give the pony its head. It will be the surer guide.

On Pennine treks, Swaledales with their white noses and black faces are likely to be seen, while in the south-west are Dartmoors with heavy fleeces almost hiding their white faces, Exmoor Horns and the various Devon breeds. Each is adapted to its environment as are the ponies described in Chapter 2.

Sheep dogs at work

One of the most interesting experiences on any trek is to watch the shepherds' dogs at work. They are controlled by a simple series of whistles, which sound unbelievably complicated where two dogs are working at once. Try and decipher them. A long drawn-out blast is the universal 'Stop' whistle. Other basic commands are 'Go Right' and 'Go Left,' and 'Come On To Your Sheep'. If you can watch each dog's response to certain whistles you will soon get the hang of it, far quicker than the dog learns to react promptly. Horse lovers are usually dog lovers, and an insight into the world of the working sheep dog is a bonus on any trekking holiday.

As Dickens said, ' 'Orses and dorgs is some men's fancy. They're wittles and drink to me'.

In spring and autumn you may see hounds at work. Your horses will certainly tell you when they are around! Foxes in hill districts must be controlled, or there would be few lambs reared, and hunting has proved the only practical means of doing this. Besides, it is great fun, and ponies that have known the excitement of the hunting field may get a bit above themselves when they hear the horn and the far cry of hound music floating across the valley, so be on your guard.

Coastal treks offer a variety of sea birds, while most mountainous districts have their local bird species. I saw my first buzzard in south Wales, my first golden eagle in Argyllshire. Try to learn from their flight, for birds are not always co-operative enough to come close enough for detailed descriptions to be useful.

The strata of rock, even the soil in a ditch changes from farm to farm and district to district. To watch them to the creak of saddle leather lends added perception. I am not sure why this should be, but doing things on horseback gives an extra dimension to life.

7 Maps and Map Reading

Maps are great fun. They are not needed on the guided trek, but buying a map of the district is still worthwhile. It is a wonderful mnemonic, bringing back memories of trekking days over the winter fire. 'Here is the corner of the wood where we made our first halt, and there the stream where Jason stumbled and splashed while crossing the ford, almost unseating Alison. That was the peak of High Scald Fell – I remember our guide said it was over 2,000ft – marked 2,256ft above sea level. Nearby are the old mine workings, right on the 2,000ft contour. What a tough life it must have been, for few days would have such clear visibility as when we looked across to the Lakeland Hills! There is Gaskill Tarn which we saw in the distance, here Mell Fell where Jewel's shoe needed attention as we stopped for a short break before completing a memorable Pennine trek.'

It is good practice to ask the morrow's route beforehand, then plot it on the map and decide the type of country. The 1-inch Ordnance is useful. Each is numbered, and the back cover shows how Great Britain is divided into 1,000 metre squares. Most back cover squares contain a sizeable town, though do not be surprised if your routes fall at the junction of a map! British Army officers claimed that every battle they fought on the North-West Frontier was uphill, before breakfast and where four maps meet, so you are in good company. A 2½-inch map is better still, showing considerably more detail. Contour marks are closer together, for while a 1-inch map may show ground of an apparently smooth slope, the 2½-inch indicates considerable unevenness en route. As yet this series does not cover the whole country. Fortunately, Ordnance Survey publish 1-inch Tourist Maps covering many of the main trekking areas. These maps include Ben Nevis and Glencoe, Dartmoor, Exmoor, Lake District, Loch Lomond and the Trossachs, New Forest, North York Moors and the Derbyshire Peak District. Ordnance Survey (Romsey Road, Maybush, Southampton SO9 4DH) supply index, catalogue and any information required. One-inch maps have a series of conventional signs, some of which, like church or chapel with tower or spire, are

Long before there was a road from Aberfoyle to the Trossachs, ponies used this track now frequented mainly by trekkers. Links with history are a common feature of treks

obvious. Others should be learned. All are listed usually at the foot of the map. The biggest danger is in confusing parish and county boundaries with footpaths and tracks.

Footpaths are marked by a series of short black dashes, whereas county boundaries are longer black dashes with more space between. County with parish or county borough boundaries are long black dashes with a dot between each. Public rights of way are indicated in red. Public bridleways are short red dashes, public footpaths are a series of red dots, while roads used as a public path are parallel black lines joined periodically in red, surmounted by a red 'w'. Untarred roads under 14 feet wide are black parallel lines with no additions. Steep gradients on roads are indicated by arrows, but these need not alarm the horseman.

Signs for marsh should be studied by the rider, as should rough pasture. Woodlands are shown green with trees depicted here and there, orchards show trees on a white ground, while bridges and footbridges are clearly marked. Of prime importance are quarries and open pits, whose signs must be learnt by heart, and checked on any route.

Other physical features listed are flat rocks, sand and mud on coasts and estuaries. Seashore riding can be marvellous, but you *must* get local sanction regarding access and safety. A 1-inch map does not differentiate between rideable and unsuitable sands.

Do not confuse national boundaries (alternate dashes and crosses) with the railway signs most of us used at school. Ordnance railways are solid black lines or alternate black and white, with circular or oblong red marks depicting stations. A red triangle is a Youth Hostel. Telephone kiosks are 'T', post offices and public houses are 'P' and 'PH' respectively, and a phone will be available at either.

Pony trekking is always liable to lead you past all sorts of historic places. A battle site is the well known crossed swords, with the date underneath (eg 1066). A castle or villa is written as such, while antiquities are shown by a black+. This must not be confused with the larger + showing the intersection of latitude and longitude at 5-minute intervals.

These degrees of latitude and longitude are shown on the map edges, and are used for finding places from a map reference. By reading off these numbers, a 4-figure reference may be plotted, using the first 2 numbers for latitude (west edge) and the second 2 for longitude (south edge). Thus the map reference for Gaskill Tarn is OS Sheet 84 (Teesdale), 2476. Such an object in such a sparsely featured countryside is easy to find from 4 figures, but precise pinpointing to within a hundred yards is possible using 6 figures. The 3rd and 6th are subdivisions into 10ths of the squares shown by 1, 2, 4 and 5. Our reading is now 246766, and positioning quick and sure.

Map scales are expressed by distance (eg on the 1-inch map, where 1 inch on the map represents 1 mile on the ground), or a Representative Fraction (1:25,000 is $2\frac{1}{2}$ inches to 1 mile, 1:63,360 is 1 inch to 1 statute mile). A linear scale may also be given at the foot of the map. Distances are measured in a straight line by ruler, or paper and pencil marks set against the linear scale. A 2p piece is 1 inch, and a hand span is a very rough guide for measuring long distances. Note your own; the average man's is around 9 inches. Width of thumb nail or little finger nail is worth knowing, as is top joint of little finger.

One kilometre is $\frac{5}{8}$ of a mile, or $\frac{10}{16}$ of an inch measured on the map. The sides of the small squares of a 1-inch map represent one kilometre.

Frequently your route will not be in a straight line. Then paper edge and pencil dots, thread, or a cheap map measuring wheel may be used. The rider must learn to relate distance to average speeds of travel. A pony's average walking speed is 4 mph or 6 when hacking.

Always read the map so that the right way up is due north. Relate it to the sun or some prominent landmark so that you are not indulging in mental contortions to decide which way west on the map really is.

Tools for safe planning

Intelligent map reading shows the nature of the topography. Contour lines are drawn every 50ft, so the closer they are, the steeper the ground. Every 250ft the contours are shown in denser line, and the highest points usually shown in feet. Heights at trigonometrical points are always marked. Some, including tourist, maps have shaded colours corresponding to a key, the darker the higher. Direction of flow in streams and rivers is another useful indication, beginning with fine lines near the source and merging into thicker patterns.

By gathering together this information, the rider is equipped to find an area suitable for planning a route, and decide the best of

several alternative means of moving from A to B. Features of special interest may be noted. Above all, use the map for safety. Avoid the worst parts of difficult country. Sensible planning will help prevent you getting lost, but if you do, the map can help you on the correct route if it is not foggy or dark.

Maps should always be folded after use in the same way they arrived from the printers: with the working surface outside. They can then be opened easily to some particular section, and folded so that only the required parts are showing. When route planning, avoid physical obstacles such as unknown river crossings, stone walls, marshes, crags, ravines, steep slopes without a path and dense woodland with no rides.

It is important not to put your mount at too steep hills unnecessarily. Having gained height, do not lose it till you must; follow the contours. Sheep tracks tend to follow contours, or if straight up and down are usually on an acceptable passage. Don't forget your horse will need a watering place from time to time, and find out whether permission is needed to pass through any part of your intended route. Allow for the type of country when planning a practical distance for each stage.

The vital route card

A route card is vital. It must include points en route, the direction of the route by compass bearings at certain stages, and distance and estimated time of arrival at each point. Make plans to deal with emergencies, accidents or bad weather. Record them on the card for this is an admirable way of implanting in your mind the type of trek on which you are about to embark.

Learning to use a compass is a great asset. The Silva type, mounted on a protractor, is recommended. Main points to bear in mind are that your position is always in the centre of a circle divided into 360 degrees. By taking an angle from north or zero, an accurate angle of direction can be measured. West bears 270 degrees from North, East bears 90 degrees, South East bears 135 degrees.

Rugged country in Perthshire. These ponies move along a clearly defined path, and a properly run trek may gain access to more country than individual riders. Ponies at the walk do far less damage to the path than when trotting or cantering

By taking bearings from the map, directions of travel may be established. Visible landmarks are used for taking bearings, and by these angles your position is plotted.

In rain, and storm which shrouds landmarks, the compass is an aid to keep your head in approximately the required direction. At no time flap the map about while mounted and do not spend time consulting it when you ought to be watching the countryside.

Very interesting treks can be made simply to practise map reading. For a start, ride to a prominent point, set the map and list grid references of all visible churches and castles, and all points or peaks over a certain altitude. From this, small groups can ride from point to point in a prescribed order, or one which they work out as best.

To practise use of the compass, riders set off to certain points and take bearings of other points from them. As they become proficient, a trek of some miles distance on compass bearings may be devised. Should bad weather make outdoor work impractical, a map reading and written question and answer session using a particular map is a valuable exercise. Confidence in map reading is an accomplishment useful in many walks of life, and the pleasantest way of attaining it is on horseback.

8 Long Distance and Post Trekking

To move on daily to a fresh camp is known as post trekking. Its attractions are more apparent than real, and in fact several competent operators have given it up. Post trekking is difficult to organise. Instead of one suitable overnight base, six are needed. The distance between them is critical to within a few miles, and frequently it will be found that some of the treks are 3 or 4 miles longer or shorter than is desirable. Hoteliers are naturally not so keen to provide accommodation and grazing for one night only, if they have the opportunity of weekly parties; hence it has off-peak possibilities.

However, it is still popular. For those who like to plan an Everest-type expedition, post trekking offers considerable scope. Daily rations must be arranged and carried. A list of equipment is needed, and costs worked out. The route must be planned in detail, using 1-inch or $2\frac{1}{2}$-inch Ordnance Survey maps. Every yard of the way needs to be checked, otherwise a wired-up gate could throw the whole expedition hours late. Rights of way, bridle paths, access to commons, open spaces and woodland must all be considered. None but fully experienced riders should contemplate such a venture.

Saddle panniers are needed to carry the day's supply of food for horse and rider. These are far better than haversacks, which tend to bounce about on the back, upsetting horse, rider and contents. Glass bottles must never be carried; plastic containers are safer, but see that no plastic bags are dropped. they can kill stock by causing a stomach obstruction.

A good average trek is 20 miles a day. Half of this should be completed before the midday break, and there is no point in attempting a big mileage and having to ride too fast or becoming so exhausted that the scenery is missed. If you want to cover a vast mileage, drive up and down a motorway.

A mounted expedition may involve carrying all feed and sleeping equipment. Sometimes an organising party arranges to meet riders at strategic points with food and tents. Sometimes a pack horse may be taken to carry such gear. This sounds a great pioneering venture, but

Post trekking in the Strathyre area of Scotland. These riders crossing the Edenample Glen put up at a different centre each night. Such ventures are only for fully experienced riders, on good ponies got into condition beforehand. All look well up to their job

it may turn into an ordinary nuisance. Two horses seldom walk at the same pace, so the pack animal is either being tugged along or held back. As it must be led in hand, the rider needs to devote attention to it throughout the day, thereby missing other facets of the route. Read early army manuals or Kipling, and you will soon discover the practical difficulties of packing. However well balanced the load at the onset, something invariably shifts.

An ordinary saddle without leathers or stirrups will do for packing. Two girths set slightly apart are recommended if practical. The War Office's Animal Management (1908) recommends:

'No load should project in such a way as to touch any part of the body; an animal should be capable of trotting and turning to either hand without being interfered with by the impedimenta, and both these tests should be employed when in doubt. A trot finds out many defects, and the attitude of the body is so different from that of a walk that parts which appear out of harm's way at the latter pace are found to be dangerously close or even touching at the trot, and especially is this true of the neck. The oscillation of the load is due to bad packing; a web surcingle should envelop the entire load and keep it secure to the animal's body and so avoid swaying.'

Equilibrium is vital. If the load is neatly halved, the animal will carry it with more ease, less expenditure of energy and with less risk of injury. It should be carried over the tops of the ribs rather than on their sides. A very high load sways backwards and forwards, and should be avoided. No load should touch the animal's body. Loads cannot be too flat: the flatter they are, the closer they lie to the saddle, giving less oscillation. Loose girths and a slack surcingle are serious evils. Army surplus ammunition bags at 25p make ideal small panniers if available.

The Duke of Edinburgh's Award Scheme issues an Expeditions Guide containing suitable menus for expedition work.

Kit for Post Trekking

The Pony Club recommends riding cap, shirt, socks and change of socks, jersey or pullover, anorak, windcheater or thick riding coat, jodhpurs or breeches and jodhpur boots or ankle boots. The ponies each require bridle with headstall and rope, saddle, saddlebags, nosebags with midday feed, and one canvas watering bucket and one hoof pick per pair. Soap, sponge and rubber curry comb or dandy brush are also required.

Each rider should have compass and maps, lightweight waterproof coat and overtrousers or hunting 'apron', nightwear, plus change of top clothing. Other recommended items are knife, fork and spoon, plastic mug, penknife, electric torch, towel and toilet articles in separate bag. A plastic groundsheet, sleeping bag and large plastic bags for spare clothes are essential when sleeping out. In this case the expedition carries its own lightweight tents, poles and pegs. Other essentials are pressure stove, fuel in polythene containers, matches, billycans and frying pan, food containers, dish cloths, water bucket, tin opener, rations and water carriers. Don't forget trowel, toilet paper, folding wash bowl and first aid kit. Needles, thread, string and pliers, spare girths and stirrup leathers, picket line and fly spray are needed. In case of foot troubles, a hammer, buffer, pincers and nails are essential. Good packing!

Riders and ponies must be fit. You cannot take a pony from a grass field and set out on a week's expedition just like that. It must have two or three months of careful training, feeding and exercise, using the saddle and the equipment to be carried. Reshoe a day or so before setting off. A reliable, fast-walking but footsure cob-type is the ideal animal, but both it and the pack pony if taken must be up to the job in hand.

Feed Requirements

Nuts, oats or other concentrates are needed. Canvas nosebags are useful for both transporting and consuming feed. They are easily made, and should be fitted so that the pony eats most of its feed without having to lower its head.

A 10-minute break in each hour is sensible. Maps must be consulted anyway, but a regular routine is best for this. Make the midday break long enough to give the ponies a real rest, and keep constant lookout for loose shoes or galling. The pack should be removed at midday, even though today's pack ponies are seldom like Kipling's camel:

> 'We packs 'im like an idol, an' you ought to 'ear 'im grunt,
> An' when we get 'im loaded up 'is blessed girth-rope breaks.'

Endurance riding is a new and very worthwhile sport in Britain. Compared with the New Countries, we tend to underestimate the horse's capabilities. Air and terrain in drier climes may favour the horse, as Hugh MacGregor explained when he many times rode 22 miles across country to see a friend's horses in Australia, returning the same evening and thinking nothing of it. An Australian stockman, with weight-distributing saddle and leading a pack animal, rode 143 miles in Victoria in 26 hours. The trail between Fort Macleod and Calgary, Alberta, is 108 miles, and this was ridden in one day by most of the Mounties and cowboys who happened to go that way. Kit Carson and five Mexican gentlemen used one saddle horse each to ride 600 miles along the Californian coast in 6 days, and only two of the party changed horses. A buckskin gelding carried a Mountie and

The end of Britain's longest trek: John o'Groat's to Land's End. Ranger looks in good shape. Note the neat saddlebag, and irons slid up the stirrup leathers now that Bill Peters has dismounted

42lb stock saddle 132 miles by sunlight from Regina to Wood Mountain Post, and bucked him off at the finish!

The Endurance Horse and Pony Society has been formed in southern England, and holds three different categories of rides. *Pleasure Rides* of 15–20 miles are non-competitive. *Competitive Trail Rides* of 25–60 miles are judged on a condition and time basis, with Junior, Novice and Open divisions. *Endurance riding* of 50–100 miles judged on the fastest fit horse carrying a minimum weight of 155lb. Ann Hyland's Arab stallion Nizzolan won the Manar trophy for the leading endurance horse of the year in 1974 and 1975.

9 Riding for the Disabled

The biggest and most unexpected pleasure of a week's trekking may be to help those less fortunate. Disabled children are having riding lessons in increasing numbers, and there is no more worthwhile way of appreciating your own fitness, if that is the case, or of learning a degree of self sufficiency if partially disabled.

The Riding for the Disabled Association (RDA) began through the inspiration afforded by Mme Liz Hartell in the 1952 Olympic Games. She won the Silver Medal for dressage, though normally chairbound with polio. Many children had been afflicted by the late 1940s polio epidemic, and it was for them that riding for the disabled was first tried.

Dr and Mrs N. Strong, South Shields, pioneered the idea in Britain, and by the late 1950s several groups had been formed. After initial scepticism, the medical profession has come down wholeheartedly on the side of this form of exercise. Basically, the pony provides four strong legs to help two less able ones, and now many types of physical disability have been eased in the saddle.

The pony's reaction is a most fascinating aspect of this venture. Its extrasensory perception is nowhere more apparent than when a well-mannered pony is brought out for a young rider who is much less than 100 per cent fit. The pony *knows*. Its pattern of behaviour is different. Helpers are constantly astonished at the way in which ponies co-operate when a disabled rider is in the saddle. Naturally, only thoroughly trustworthy ponies are used, but the animals themselves have played a large part in persuading 'non-horsey' nurses and doctors that here is a real boon for their charges.

When RDA began its work, the horse world seemed more of a closed shop than today. People naturally queried whether a big, strong animal was in fact suited to the needs of someone normally confined to a wheelchair. Today very carefully controlled conditions are used, and are now standard through all the 296 member groups. Ponies are sometimes borrowed from individual owners, or hired. Often riding schools and trekking centres make the splendid gesture of lending mounts free of charge, and where this is coupled with use of covered riding school, the very maximum benefit is gained by disabled riders. Rain is their enemy in riding sessions, hence the invaluable part played by covered facilities.

In addition to ponies, helpers are needed. Up to three per pony are required, one to lead the animal and one on each side to steady the rider. Pressure of applications is such that the more severely disabled are given pride of place. With this level of assistance and a quiet mount, riding is often possible for the people who are too badly handicapped to manage other, basically simpler exercises.

Riding gives a sense of independence and temporary relief from the frustrations felt by physically handicapped people. They appreciate looking *down* on someone for a change! Once in the saddle, they are horsemen, just the same as any other rider. To exercise control over a large animal is an incentive to someone whose own bodily functions are limited, and the skills acquired constantly surprise instructors. Backs straighten and heads are held still, sometimes for the first time. Riding has thus been shown to contribute to physical improvement through providing a new incentive, but its most valuable contribution is by providing enjoyment and a sense of achievement. It makes a positive link with the able bodied world.

In *Action*, the magazine of the National Fund for Research into Crippling Diseases, Geoffrey Brooke wrote:

'Children provide most of the RDA's riders and to watch a session is a fascinating experience. Sometimes the children are collected from individual homes, but more often they come from a hospital or school for the handicapped. Arriving with a full outfit of crutches, braces and wheelchairs they seem uniformly pale and rather quiet: until they see the ponies, when eyes light up and chatter breaks out. They are helped from off the vehicles and then walked, carried or propelled to their steeds and fitted with a belt (useful in emergencies) and a riding cap.

'Some are then lifted onto their ponies – a few may be able to mount without assistance – while the rest wait their turn in a row of wheelchairs.'

A qualified riding instructor is always at hand, but there are never too many helpers. Here is an outlet providing the best means of

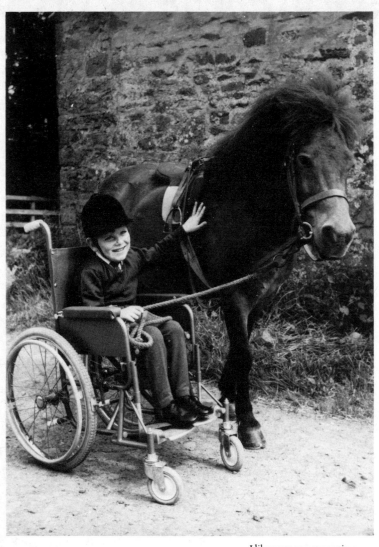

I like my pony at any time . . .

. . . but best of all when I'm on top!

showing gratitude for a fit body, both for a short spell during the trekking week if opportunity arises, or regularly through the rest of the year. Men are always in special demand to do the lifting, as most helpers are women. Mounting apparatus has been devised to help overcome this difficulty.

Princess Anne is RDA's Patron. She visits groups in action, and her interest is a stimulus to others to help this most deserving cause. Only two of RDA's members work full time. Though over 6,000 physically and mentally handicapped people benefit from RDA's work, 50 times that number could be helped if facilities, ponies and helpers were available. Remember, you do not need experience with horses or riding to help; energy, enthusiasm and the ability to run are the main attributes.

Apart from actively assisting with ponies and riders, help in transporting riders or ponies is needed. Another aspect is organising helpers by letter or phone, or planning a crèche for helpers' children.

Could you found a new group in your area? Or help with a riding holiday, or at a county or horse show stand? Few things are more rewarding. There have been startling 'before and after' cases, like the small boy who took his first unaided steps towards the pony he was about to ride, and another who had never spoken before he was heard talking to his mount. RDA do not stress these successes; they wish to avoid raising false hopes; but the work they do is worthy of support from all.

Young Exmoors

10 Instructors and Operators

What Makes a Good Instructor?

Three grades of instructor are recognised by the British pony authorities. Grade I is competent to take complete charge of a pony trekking centre. Grade II is competent to take charge of a pony trekking centre under the supervision of the operator. Grade III is a competent rider, able to take charge of a trek.

The road to recognition as a trek instructor is more clearly marked than 20 years ago, but it is nevertheless a hard one. The only person of use to an operator is one who can take charge of a trek. There is no in-between, 'odd-job' stage. Therefore you must gain experience somehow. One method is to pay as a guest, but to help the instructor in any way possible. You are dealing not only with horses but with humans, often the more awkward of the two! The fact that you own a pony and have fed, groomed and ridden it for some years may help, but looking after a string of ponies is a very different matter. It is physically tiring, even exhausting. You must be tough and capable, working and making decisions before and after the actual trek. Really keen riders have found that they just could not cope with the sheer numbers of mounts, tack and guests involved.

Even if fully qualified as a rider and capable of caring for guests, an instructor from another district needs a full fortnight to learn the country. It is vital to know the routes, local weather signs, relationships with neighbouring farmers, keepers and landowners. Meal break places and times between the different points must become as familiar as the ponies and their idiosyncrasies. These things can only be learned when trekkers are actually there; it is of no use helping in the more leisurely out-of-season atmosphere.

A week's intensive course for pony trekking instructors is now available in Scotland and Wales. Such courses fill a great need. Leading operators would like to see a Government grant towards this vital educational aspect, rather than assistance with establishing the centres themselves. The oral and practical examination at the end of the course gives a good idea of its content.

The best way to learn about tack. In the open, with ponies on either hand, this young lady has an early lesson on how to buckle bits onto bridles. The ponies are well separated, as they should be during breaks

Notes for the Guidance of Pony Trekking Leaders and *Guide to Pony Trekking Operators* are compulsory reading, as is *The Highway Code* where it refers to horses and horsemen. There must be a knowledge of the countryside, country manners and the Country Code. First Aid must be learned, the British Red Cross Society's Junior Manual being a good guide.

In addition to mounting and dismounting correctly, candidates must be able to walk, trot, and canter, and lead another pony from the saddle. They must display assurance and dexterity in the saddle.

On the subject of horsemanship, candidates must know the points of the horse and its conformation, must possess a general knowledge of British breeds and types, and their suitability for trekking and trail riding. Feeding, watering, health, housing and shelter, grooming, shoeing and tying up are included. Knowledge of tack and its fitting is vital, as is elementary veterinary knowledge. Questions on trek organisation and management cover ponies, staff and facilities, organisation of a trek, responsibility to riders and operators, and trekkers' welfare, accommodation and entertainment. Routes, access and countryside behaviour are also queried.

It cannot be over-stressed that trek instructors must like people as well as horses. They must have a sense of humour as well as of responsibility. In addition to being sound riders themselves, they must be able to impart knowledge to guests – how to mount and dismount, and the right way to sit at all paces, whether uphill or down. Being confident themselves, they must give confidence to the most nervous of guests. This is vital. When working daily among horses for years on end, it is easy to forget that people brought up in towns may have had no contact with animals of any sort. On no account must an instructor scoff at the timid attempts of a tyro: a little experience teaches that the most nervous beginners often blossom out into competent riders in a remarkably short space of time.

A sensible standard of behaviour must be insisted on for the sake of other riders. This may involve toning down the 'cowboy' or know-all, for the leader must *lead*. There should never be any doubt about who is in charge, and this involves some tactful orders when safety is at stake. Anyone liable to get in a flap when things go wrong should not consider the post of trek leader.

A knowledge of local history is an asset, as is information about the farms, trees, ruins and streams passed en route. An instructor with a flair for organising games and dancing in the evenings is an asset to any centre. Even more important is respect for local people going about their daily work. To greet locals pleasantly may sound obvious good manners, but a mounted position at the head of a trek has been known to go to the instructor's own head!

The instructor decides when and where to stop for a meal break. He or she must see that the ponies are hobbled, let loose or tied up, for guests do not like an indecisive person in charge. Some riders may need help, especially early in the week, even with loosening a girth. If saddles are taken off, they should be laid the correct way up: pommel to the ground. When resuming, saddles and bridles must be put on correctly, and correctly adjusted. It is part of the instructor's job to spot whether guests look 'happy' in the saddle.

Pony trekking people are seldom litter louts, but an important duty of the instructor is to check that all is tidy after meal break. No piece of paper or orange peel must be left in sight; there should be no more evidence of the trek's passing than a few hoof marks.

To show guests how to groom, the instructor must himself be adept. Feeding must be supervised, and each horse's condition noted frequently until it becomes a matter of course. 'Is Gypsy as fit as she was last week, or has she lost a bit of flesh?' Ponies cannot be fed to any precise scale; amounts needed to keep them in optimum condition vary between individuals and times of the year. Any lameness during the trek should be noticed immediately, and sometimes the horse may have to be walked. If practical, the guest should take the instructor's horse, while the latter walks with the lame one.

Proper ways of cleaning tack must be thoroughly understood. Guests must be taught how to take it apart, and to reassemble it in proper order. Reasons for cleanliness must be explained, even simple things like caked sweat on girths causing soreness.

The instructor should know the phone number of the nearest doctor and vet. A first aid kit must be carried. If in doubt, he should consult the operator. Above all, loyalty to the operator is expected. Much hard work has gone into organising a season's trekking, as well as a great deal of money.

Operators and the Law

Under the Riding Establishments Act 1964, all pony trekking centres must be licensed. It is illegal to run a riding centre of any kind, where horses are hired in any way, without a licence from the County Council concerned. First step is to send for application forms. These must be returned with a fee of £10, which applies annually. Operators must re-apply; they do not get automatic renewal. Not so long ago the fee was 10 shillings!

Operators must satisfy the County Council on three counts. Their Fire Officer will inspect premises, while a vet on the Council's panel inspects horses. A Land Agent makes a general assessment. One acre of grazing per pony is recommended. Advertising may start once the licence is granted.

Insurance is compulsory. Minimum cover of £100,000 against accidents or injuries to trekkers, ponies, or other people and their property is a condition of the licence, and costs some £30 a year.

Britain has 4,000 riding centres, and 25 per cent of them are sub-standard. These facts come from 'Ponies of Britain', who should know, as they inspect and register suitable centres. They check up on general cleanliness, tidiness, supervision of unaccompanied children, and that most important character, atmosphere.

'Ponies of Britain' do a first-class inspecting job. The more competent operators would like a grading system on the lines of AA and RAC hotel starring. An experienced instructor may be engaged by the licensee to run the trek, but such a person must be over 17 years of age.

Even though the operator may employ a trek leader, he is laying out his own money on ponies, and these must be of suitable type. Good temperament is essential. The ponies must be up to their job, capable of carrying a rider of a certain weight range. The pony's height is no guarantee of its suitability; bone, substance and general conformation are far more important. For instance, the genuine old-fashioned type of 13.2 hands Welsh pony will carry an average man all day, whereas a more highly bred show type of the same height will not.

'Ponies of Britain' stress constantly the dangers and cruelties of using very young ponies. Trekking ponies should be at least 4 years old. If they are rideable by novices at a younger age, the reason is usually poverty and its attendant weakness. The ponies simply lack the strength to play up. Individual ponies may have such equable temperaments that any child can do anything with them, but even in such isolated cases the bones and muscles are immature. A pony ridden too early develops a compressed spine, which looks (and is) horrific on X-ray. Icelandic ponies are popular with centres for this reason; they are not ridden until 4 or even 5 years old, and then last a great many years. A hill pony that has not been too 'humanised' is best. By this I mean that the pony has been reared for 3 years or so on the hill, and does not meet his first contact with discipline until rounded up for breaking. He still has his independence; he will not walk into a bog or a wire fence not knowing what they are, or put his nose inside every bucket expecting to be provided for without effort. Irish ponies are good in this respect; they have learnt to live among bog and rock, and would not have survived at all if they lacked a strong constitution.

If a weekly intake of 20 guests is planned, it is of no use procuring 20 ponies. One spare per 5 ponies is required: if 20 are going out daily, the total stable must number at least 25. No animal should be worked when sick or lame, but when guests are paying the bill they expect ponies to ride on, hence the spares.

Operators and instructors must know their ponies. They should be able to decide speedily which to allocate to which guest. Simple tasks soon indicate new riders' handiness or otherwise, and a ham-fisted individual should be allocated a sluggish or rather stubborn pony that he is unlikely to harm. Usually someone of reliable character and previous riding experience can be mounted on the first pony of the string, so that the instructor operates independently, and moves along the line as circumstances dictate. This lead pony is vital. It should be a free-walking, even-tempered individual, not given to peeping sideways at everything it passes. If the lead pony steps away and looks straight ahead, the chances are that the rest will follow suit. If, however, you choose as leader a sprightly but temperamental pony that seeks something strange behind every wall and tree, the rest will do the same, like the copycats they are.

Having bought the ponies and settled them in order for the first trek, both operator and instructor must note the condition of the string. Some ponies thrive on lots of work and little feed; others are the reverse. One animal may go through the season with no break, another may need a week or two's rest just when the centre is busiest. Constant watch must be kept for saddle sores and girth galls, the commonest cause of having to lay off a pony. All ponies must be watched for lameness. A comprehensive first-aid kit for both ponies and trekkers must be kept at the centre, and a smaller kit taken on treks.

A sensible, competent rider should also take the rear. This person can watch what is happening all along the line, can shut gates and keep the string reasonably compact. It is of course the instructor's *responsibility* to see that all gates are closed. With good lead and rear riders, only one instructor is needed, and this is a better system than having a large string with two. One instructor has sole responsibility; if there are two, and if something goes wrong, one may try to shift blame onto the other.

Lunch places are prearranged by the operator. Water, grazing, pleasant surroundings and natural conveniences for riders are desirable. Do not allow ponies to be tied direct to a fence by their halters. One pony pulling back upsets others and may break the fence. A light and easily broken string connecting fence with halter rope is better, but hobbles are best of all.

Arranging Adequate Feed

All ponies need supplementary feed when trekking. However good the grass, it does not suffice, due to a combination of the energy used when walking up to 20 miles, and the reduced grazing period between treks. A trekking pony needs rest as well as feed. If it is given no concentrates, it must spend its time trying to fill itself from the grass, thereby using still more energy and getting short of rest. A concentrate feed on being caught in the morning, and another at night before turning out to pasture, are the minimum. Overfeeding can be as serious as underfeeding, and weigh scales are only a guide, because individuals vary so. Observation is necessary, and while not wishing to make a mystique of feeding, it cannot be overstressed that the successful feeding of a string of trekking ponies depends very much on the eye of the operator. If grazing is poor, hay may be needed even in summer, especially in a southern drought. If ponies 'tuck up' and lose flesh on their quarters, the chances are that bulk is insufficient, and hay is needed.

Chop (chopped hay or oasts in the sheaf), crushed oats and bran fed slightly damped make a good feed. A feed is necessary at midday unless there is ample good grazing round about, and the supplement must be either carried or sent on ahead. Ponies are jealous at feeding time: they must be spread well apart, or kicking and biting occurs. Cubes or nuts are a convenient form of concentrate, and a reliable brand contains necessary trace elements and minerals.

These minerals are vital to maintain health. Salt, bonemeal or proprietary mineral mixtures are all useful. A lump of rock salt was left in every manger in the old workhorse stables. Horses lose a lot of salt in their sweat, and this must be made up. When ponies are sweating a lot, one ounce of salt daily should be added to the ration.

Despite adequate diet, ponies may remain in poor condition. In such cases, dose for worms, using doses obtained from your vet or agricultural chemist. Teeth defects occur with the same result of poor condition, and are a case for the vet.

Ponies should never be left short of water. If water bowls or buckets are not supplied in stalls, ponies should be led out and watered several times a day. Watering *before* feeds is the rule, or the feed may be swilled out of the stomach.

Winter Problems

Wintering is a difficult problem for the trekking operator. If expensive, it may swallow up summer profits. If badly done, the ponies will not be fit for the new season. One golden rule is never to sell out in autumn and try to buy back in next spring. No reputable operator would contemplate such a policy, but it is done, buying ponies as cheaply as possible and selling later for what they will fetch. Ponies are always dearer in spring, consequently anyone trying to buy on the cheap is dealing in third-rate stock.

A good policy is to lend ponies to reliable homes, *not* to commercial establishments. After a summer's trek, every pony deserves a rest, not a winter in a riding school. Ponies may have to be delivered, and picked up again from places known or recommended to the operator. 'Meat for work' is the basis of this bargain. As riding is possible only at weekends and holidays during the short winter days, ponies are seldom over-ridden.

When wintered at home, a well sheltered field with ample water is needed. Natural shelter and a residue of rough grazing form the ideal combination, but hay should be given early in the winter to maintain condition. Autumn grass is seldom as good as it looks. Once a pony loses condition in winter, you cannot put it back on again before spring, however expensive the feed. Even when ponies are not fed, they should be inspected daily by someone who can spot trouble before it develops.

'As the day lengthens, so the cold strengthens', and March, and April in the north, are very difficult months for outlying stock. Extra feeding is necessary to combat night frosts and east winds.

Though ponies are turned away with their shoes off, they must be inspected regularly, and hoofs trimmed where necessary during the winter. A full week before trekking starts they must be brought in from wintering. They must receive one working feed a day, be given a good clean up, and shod all round. They must learn that after a winter of freedom, the time for discipline has arrived.

During summer, feet must be inspected regularly. Ponies on regular treks need shoeing every four or five weeks, but this varies with the ground and the individual pony. Sometimes it is only necessary to remove the shoes, dress the feet, and replace. A smith can usually be found for the comparatively large numbers involved, but operator and instructors must be familiar with shoeing routine, and be able to take off a loose shoe, even if they cannot replace it.

Servicing the Tack

That other country craftsman, the saddler, is also in short supply. If there is none locally, extra tack must be kept to make up for time lag in repairs. A few stitches can make the difference between a safe saddle, bridle or stirrup leather, and one which causes an accident, putting someone off riding for life if not injuring the rider.

Good tack is not cheap. There are foreign saddles which look smart, but which do not have the life of English leather, and are difficult if not impossible to repair. Saddles should fit the individual animal, and be kept for that pony and no other. Watch throughout the season to ensure that the saddles still fit. As the padding flattens or moves, a saddle that fitted at Easter may press on the pony's back by midsummer. Saddle trees will become cracked or broken through

Hugh MacGregor leads a trek of instructors at Aberfoyle. A full week's course takes place in March, and is a great opportunity for exchanging views and ways and means of keeping pony trekking up to date

careless use. Girth straps wear; when one becomes unsafe it should not be used until it is mended. A lot of broken or worn saddlery is off-putting to guests and will certainly cause an inspector to fail the centre.

Tack should be cleaned thoroughly at least once a week, and inspected by the person in charge. Teach guests to look for developing faults. It is an essential part of horsemanship, and the operator who looks to the future and not merely to the present week is the one who will succeed. Stirrup leathers should also be inspected weekly, paying particular attention to the stitching, which may become worn or cut, and therefore dangerous.

If a guest complains about a saddle, investigate the complaint. It may be human weakness due to unaccustomed exercise, but equally possibly the saddle may be at fault.

Every trekking centre should have a good supply of stirrup irons. Small irons which nip the feet are highly dangerous, and a number of 5-inch irons should be on hand to accommodate the heavy footwear often favoured by male riders. Small irons and short leathers should also be available for small children.

Many centres regard a head collar as ideal equipment. It is dual-purpose. A rope or shank running through the D-ring at the back of the jaw, and tied round the pony's neck with a *non-slip* knot, is there for any occasion that may arise during the day. The pony can be tied up in the stall or on the trek, and is more easily caught if turned loose to graze. Reins and bit are attached to the head collar when the trek is due to start, and are taken off at lunch. Reins and bridles are less likely to be broken by this system.

Some centres are going over to Western saddles. In these, a long stirrup is used, and the rider simply sits in the saddle rather than moving with the horse's motion as in English style. These saddles are expensive, costing £100 or over, but they do last.

Otherwise an English leather saddle is best. Foreign ones should be avoided, as they are by no means well built, and can soon cause sores. No two saddles are the same, any more than any two horses' backs are exactly alike, and when a saddle has been found to fit a pony perfectly, it should be used for no other. The name should be clearly marked in the harness room.

A thick, fleecy saddle cloth should be used on every ride. There are

Trekkers in the sun. Wales offers an excellent variety of riding country. Saddle cloths as seen here should always be used.

varying types, including some serviceable ones of man-made fibre, or from layers of anorak material.

The Western bridle requires a very light bit, so is *not* suitable for novices. An ordinary snaffle bridle is best. It should rest on the space in the horse's mouth where teeth are absent. If too high it will curl up the lips, and if too low will rest on the teeth. A pony needing anything more severe than the snaffle bit is unsuitable for novice riders and trekking.

Costly though it is, the qualities which Will H. Ogilvie found in English leather remain:

> 'Long before the great World-War,
> When we sought in Sunny Land
> From the little township store
> Girth or bridle, strap or band,
> If we wanted it to stand
> Strain of work or stress of weather
> Yet be kindly to the hand,
> We would ask for "English leather".'

Appendix 1

The Countryside and the Law

The countryside is the farmer's business premises, as author A. G. Street was fond of telling us. When riding anywhere in Britain, the fundamental rule at all times is that the land belongs to someone. Common land is not common to everyone. It covers a million acres in England, and half a million in Wales; there is no common land in Scotland. The term itself has no precise definition. The Royal Commission on Common Land 1955–8 recognised eight different categories of common land. Even when several adjoining farms graze sheep on a single common, that land is usually owned by another individual, and it must never be taken for granted that you have a legal right to ride over any wide open space. *Nor does being in a National Park change the laws of access in any way.*

If you ride from a recognised trekking centre, the guides will know where they may go. I have yet to meet a farmer who disliked seeing others on the land provided they were acting responsibly. It is avoidable silliness like leaving gates open and dumping litter which causes ill feeling, in some cases to the extent that the innocent suffer with the guilty. The only sensible plan is to find out beforehand where you may go and where riding is barred.

It never pays to 'get on one's high horse' in the countryside. Some byroads are access roads to farms. You may have perfect legal right to use them, but do so in such a fashion as not to cause extra work. Rights of way often pass through farm yards. Again, remember that the farmer will probably have to spend his time and money repairing holes made by a hundred hoofs several times a week. Proprietors of the best trekking centres actively assist farming; they put up a new gate at the wood corner, fill in ruts by the ford, replace several rails in a fence where a pony broke only one.

This spirit of co-operation makes a happier atmosphere all round. Shepherds and farmers are quite often interested in horses, and so are basically sympathetic to your activities. *Don't* spoil this bond with thoughtless actions. Over open moor, stick to the tracks. Grouse are a very valuable asset on heather, and seldom do you know they are there till you actually disturb them. The keeper's fear is that they will be driven to a different section of the moor, possibly onto another beat, and he will have little sport to show his employer. *Don't interfere with snares if you see any*. Keepers are responsible for vermin control, and the cruel gin trap is now forbidden in England and Wales.

There may be access agreements for woodland. Forests in Britain are owned either by the Forestry Commission, investment groups or private estates. Forest riding has the advantage of safety, for the bulldozed tracks are easy to follow, and the narrowness of the way helps supervision. It can become boring when acre after acre of spruce is passed, but this is seldom the case where private landlords are concerned. As taxpayers we spend many millions of pounds on the Forestry Commission and investment companies, so the rider has a right to ask permission to use their woods. This does not mean that it will always be granted.

Mr D. W. Henman, Forestry Commission District officer at Aberfoyle, Perthshire, is in charge of four forests lying between Loch Tay, Loch Lomond, River Clyde and Bridge of Allen. He is an enthusiastic advocate of properly conducted trekking through forests. Though pony trekking and walking do not go too well together, as ponies leave soft muddy places which walkers do not like, there is plenty of space for both in the forests:

'Pony trekking is right in line with Forestry Commission policy on enjoyment of the countryside. It is quiet enjoyment, nothing to do with petrol engines, and activities like bird watching and picnics can be done in conjunction with it. A well-organised trek is easier for us to deal with than are individual riders, as the trekking operator is held responsible should any damage occur. If individual riders get out of hand, it is less easy for us to pin-point the blame, and the same applies to walkers who cannot be traced.'

Local people may get permission to ride in the forests, but this has to be positively granted. One horse cantering can do more harm than a score at the walk, and is also more liable to ride into forbidden areas. Post trekking is also allowed over these Perthshire forests, for the hilltops are often left unplanted because of exposure, and make good riding country. Because of fire hazard, Forestry Commission roads have to be a certain width, which make better riding than narrow tracks. There is the danger that the picking action of the ponies' feet will start potholes in graded dry metalled roads, in which case the trek may be restricted to verges, or barred from certain roads.

Byways include many different categories. Provided they exercise proper care and attention, horsemen are permitted to ride on public rights of way, bridleways, drove roads, and permitted rights of way for horsemen. These rights of way are marked in the local county and district council offices. If such a right of way is obstructed, by a wired-up gate, fallen tree, broken bridge or poor drainage, then notify the local authority, who have the task of maintenance.

The law on straying stock has changed lately. A horse owner is liable to prosecution if a horse or pony strays unattended on a public road. He is liable for damages if an accident is caused to any person because his animal is not under proper control.

Appendix 2

The Country Code

1 Guard against fire risks
2 Fasten all gates
3 Keep dogs under proper control (allow no dogs on the trek)
4 Keep to paths across farm land
5 Avoid damaging fences, hedges and walls
6 Leave no litter
7 Safeguard water supplies
8 Protect wild life, wild plants and trees
9 Go carefully on country roads
10 Respect the life of the countryside

Appendix 3

Some Useful Addresses

CONNEMARA PONY BREEDERS'
  SOCIETY
J. Killeen Esq
4 Nun's Island
Galway
Eire
(Tel. Galway 091-32-77)

DALES PONY SOCIETY
G. H. Hodgson Esq
Ivy House Farm
Yarm-on-Tees
Yorkshire

DARTMOOR PONY SOCIETY
D. W. J. O'Brien Esq
Chelwood Farm
Nutley
Uckfield
Sussex
(Tel. Chelwood Gat 251)

ENGLISH CONNEMARA PONY SOCIETY
Mrs Barthrop
The Quinta
Bentley
Farnham
Surrey
(Tel. Bentley 3159)

EXMOOR PONY SOCIETY
Mrs J. Watts
Quarry Cottage
Sampford Brett
Williton
Somerset
(Tel. Williton 539)

FELL PONY SOCIETY
Miss P. Crossland
Packway
Windermere
Westmorland
(Tel. Windermere 3152)

THE HAFLINGER SOCIETY
Miss J. Evers-Swindell
Bron-y-Craig
Pwyllglas
Ruthin
Denbighshire

HIGHLAND PONY SOCIETY
J. McLldowie Esq
Dunblane
Perthshire

NEW FOREST PONY AND CATTLE
  BREEDING SOCIETY
Miss D. Macnair
Beacon Corner
Burley
Ringwood
Hants
(Tel. Burley 2272)

SHETLAND PONY STUD BOOK
D. M. Patterson Esq
8 Whinfield Road
Montrose
Angus
(Tel. Montrose 683)

WELSH PONY AND COB SOCIETY
T. E. Roberts Esq
32 North Parade
Aberystwyth
Cards
(Tel. Aberystwyth 2924)

ASSOCIATION OF BRITISH RIDING
    SCHOOLS
The Secretary
Chesham House
56 Green End Road
Sawtery
Hants
(Tel. Ramsey 830278)

BRITISH FIELD SPORTS SOCIETY
26 Caxton Street
London SW1
(Tel. 01-222-5407)

BRITISH HAY & STRAW MER-
    CHANTS ASSOCIATION
F. W. Burton Esq
70 Wigmore Street
London W1
(Tel. 01-935-8534)

BRITISH VETERINARY ASSOCIATION
7 Mansfield Street
Portland Place
London W1
(Tel. 01-636-6541)

NATIONAL MASTER FARRIERS' AND
    BLACKSMITHS' ASSOCIATION
674 Leeds Road
Lofthouse Gate
Wakefield
(Tel. Wakefield 823286)

NATIONAL PONY SOCIETY
Commodore B. H. Brown RN
    (Ret'd)
Stoke Lodge
85 Cliddesden Road
Basingstoke
Hants
(Tel. Basingstoke 22906)

PONIES OF BRITAIN CLUB
Brookside Farm
Ascot
Berks

RIDING FOR THE DISABLED ASSO-
    CIATION
Miss C. M. L. Haynes
Avenue 'R'
National Agricultural Centre
Kenilworth
Warks
(Tel. Coventry 56107)

WESTERN HORSEMAN'S ASSOCIATION
Round Close
Yately
Camberley
Surrey

Appendix 4

Going Metric with Maps

The Ordnance Survey published the first metric 1:50,000 maps in 1974 This first issue covers Britain south of a line drawn just north of York. The 1:50,000 maps of northern Britain should be available from 1976. The 1-inch sheets (1-93) are still available (1976), but once all metric maps are published they will disappear. It is important to note that the sheet numbers and sheet boundaries of the 1:50,000 series do not coincide with the 1-inch sheets, so always check that you are getting the sheet you want.

The 1:50,000 series of Ordnance Survey maps is to a slightly larger scale than the 1-inch series, so detail is easier to read. A number of important changes in design and colour will be of relevance to the practical map reader. There are 204 1:50,000 sheets, instead of 189 1-inch sheets, each being larger, though covering a smaller area. The Grid colour is now blue and motorways are shown in blue; B roads and contours have changed from brown to orange, housing is now shaded with orange stipple. A very noticeable change is the omission of black tree symbols, woodland being shown with green shading so this means having to wait and see whether woodland will be deciduous or coniferous.

The contours on the new maps are labelled in metres. On the First Series this may be confusing, as the interval is still 50ft. In the Second Series the contours will be arranged more regularly but for the present they are shown to nearest metre. The main problem for the map user is that the countour values in metres appear irregular. Care is needed in checking the relief of the land.

Most symbols on the 1:50,000 maps are straightforward and closely related to the 1-inch symbols. There has been some concern about confusion of paths and county or parish boundaries in some areas. This was always a problem and careful map-reading is important. As the county councils produced their definitive public rights of way information the Ordnance Survey introduced new symbols to indicate public rights of way on the 1-inch map. These symbols can be found on the new maps too. Please note that any path or track shown on the maps unless in the new red path symbols is not evidence of a right of way.

Public rights of way are shown by three symbols: footpaths by red dotted line; bridleways by red-pecked line; road used as a public footpath or byway open to all traffic, red pecked line with red dots on alternating sides.

For greater detail and accuracy the 1:25,000 maps are now appearing in their first full edition although most of the country is covered by the provisional edition. Apart from a larger scale these maps show every field boundary.

Appendix 5

Trekking Centres

This is a brief selection from the list of over 160 trekking and riding holiday centres approved by 'Ponies of Britain'. The full list is available from 'Ponies of Britain', Brookside Farm, Ascot, Berkshire, price 35p (send stamped addressed envelope). Charges quoted are approximate: they are always subject to change and often depend on individual requirements. *Neither 'Ponies of Britain' nor the publishers are responsible for them*: apply direct to the centre for accurate information. Our random list in no way implies superiority over other Ponies of Britain Centres.

England

OLD MILL STABLES, Lelant Downs, Hayle, Cornwall. Tel: Hayle 3045. Principals: the Misses M. Scotting and S. Renowden. RESIDENTIAL in very comfortable private house in Lelant village for those of 21 and over. Guests transported to and from the stables and from the station at a nominal extra charge. Good cooking, homely, double rooms with H & C. Also country cottage accommodation 2 miles distant of similar standard. Hotel accommodation also available. Sheltered caravan and camping site 5 minutes' walk away. Children taken for daily rides only. Elementary instruction given to all stages. Separate riding holiday for all stages of rider; beginners and experienced do not ride together. Open for riding holidays from end of March to end of June and month of September, but lessons and hacking are available all the year round. No riders taken over the weekends, but guests may arrive on Saturday. Weight limit 12½ stone. For terms apply direct. Highly Recommended.

COLWILL, MRS C., 'Littlecombe', Holne, Ashburton, Devon. Tel: Poundsgate 260. RESIDENTIAL for 3 people at most, sensible teenagers from 14 yrs old and adults who enjoy a quiet country life. Mrs Colwill has long practical experience and only keeps 12 horses and ponies. A small quiet centre. Weekly bookings from Saturday to Sunday, weekend riding when not fully booked – and daily riding when ponies are available. Camping facilities for small groups, and space for one caravan with family on the farm who may ride daily or as they wish. Accommodation at nearby farmhouse. Highly Recommended.

LONG-DISTANCE RIDING, run by Miss J. P. Davies, Mead House, Rissington Road, Bourton-on-the-Water, Gloucestershire. Tel: Bourton-on-the-Water 20358. NON-RESIDENTIAL. A livery and training centre second to none. Riders are accommodated at the Old Fosseway Hotel, $\frac{1}{4}$ mile away, which is good with a friendly atmosphere, and unaccompanied children (supervised) or children with non-riding parents at nearby guest house. Children are well occupied at the centre from 9.30 am to 6.0 pm. Accommodation at local houses when hotel is full. Terms on application. There is a 4-day course in long-distance riding *for 5 competent riders only from 10 years of age* during school holidays at £25. *Riders must bring their own ponies.* Adult courses (riders bringing their own ponies) especially designed for the Golden Horseshoe Ride are held in early spring, other courses in late summer or autumn. Highly Recommended.

KNOWLE RIDING CENTRE, Knowle House, Timberscombe, Somerset. Tel: Timberscombe 342. Prop: John R. Lamacraft. RESIDENTIAL at Knowle House, an attractive large house standing in its own grounds, with stabling and paddocks attached, or at nearby hotels and inns, notably the Luttrell Arms, Dunster (AA**). Terms: Ordinary Riding Holiday (morning rides only) £45 per week. Full Riding Holiday (longer rides) £50 per week. Non-Riding Holiday £35 per week. Extra riding by the hour. No riding on Saturdays or Sunday afternoons during high season period except at Easter and Whitsun. Reduction for children under 11 sharing parents' room. Unaccompanied children of 12 years and over taken. Highly Recommended.

SURREY CREST RIDING HOLIDAY CENTRE, North Park Lane, Godstone, Surrey. Tel: Godstone 2715. Prop: Miss Pat Kellaway. RESIDENTIAL in timber buildings fitted with electricity, instant hot water and modern sanitation, each containing 6 two-bedded rooms. Also chalets sleeping two or three persons. Baths always available and basins in each room. Club room for discussions, lectures, and indoor games. Unaccompanied children from 8 yrs (supervision at all times), adults and families taken. Riding daily over downland, instruction by qualified staff if required, lectures, stable management and competitions. Weekly holidays, 8–16 yrs from £40–45, 16 yrs and over from £45–50, deposit of £18 on booking. Weekends 8–16 yrs from £12, 16 yrs and over from £14, deposit of £6 on booking. Approved by the Association of British Riding Schools whose tests will be taken. Highly Recommended.

Scotland

GLENESK PONY TREKKING CENTRE, Dalbrack, Tarfside, Brechin, Angus. Tel: Tarfside 233. Props: Mr and Mrs McIntosh. RESIDENTIAL farmhouse, 12 miles from Edzell, 20 miles from Brechin. Good trekking on Highland type ponies over the Dalhousie Estate hill paths. Escorted by guide. Suitable for families and young people. No unaccompanied children under 14 yrs old taken. Accommodation in 3- or 4-bedded rooms. Good food and friendly atmosphere with delightful, homely Scottish farmer and his wife. Terms from £40 + VAT per week in low season. Double-bedded room £2 extra per person. Guests can be met by arrangement at Montrose Station or Brechin bus stance (both 20-mile journeys) at a charge of £1.25 per head per journey. A good centre: Highly Recommended.

TROSSACHS HOTEL, By Callander, Perthshire. A famous AA*** hotel situated in very beautiful surroundings on the shores of Loch Achray in the heart of the Trossachs. Trekking organised by Mr Hugh McGregor, one of the best operators, undertaken on first-class Highland ponies, under a competent trek leader/guide. About 14 to 16 ponies. An ideal centre in ideal surroundings. For terms apply direct to Mr Hugh McGregor, Ballinton, Thornhill, Stirling. Trekking for persons from 17 yrs of age. Give previous experience if any. This is a lively centre, and crowded in the season. Also water ski-ing, dinghy sailing, fishing, private tennis courts, billiards room, library, TV, dancing almost every evening, and cocktail bar. Highly Recommended.

Wales

DWYFOR WELSH COB STUD RIDING AND TREKKING CENTRE, Llanystumdwy, Criccieth, Caernarvonshire. Tel: Criccieth 2397. Props: Mr and Mrs Tysilio Jones. RESIDENTIAL in Dwyfor Ranch Hotel and in modern self-catering cabins for 4 or 6 persons. Hotel accommodation (list and charges sent on request). One week's Instructional Riding £28, Day Course (during low season) £6.50; indoor school. Hourly hacking £2. Weekend riding. Liveries, breaking and schooling. The centre is 1½ miles west of Criccieth on the Pwllheli road and has 60–70 horses. Tennis courts, golf course, bowling green, fishing, boating. Non-riders and children welcome; families catered for, but *not unaccompanied children under 16 yrs of age.* Open from April. Recommended.

GARTHEWIN FARM PONY TREKKING CENTRE, Llanfair Talhaiarn, nr Abergele, Denbighshire. Tel: Llanfair Talhaiarn 288. Props: Mr & Mrs Farquhar MacBain. NON-RESIDENTIAL, but family-type accommodation available in large country house (2- 3- and 4-bedded rooms); bed, breakfast, packed lunch and evening meal £25 per week + £2 VAT, £4 per day + 32p VAT. Bed and breakfast only £2.50 per day + 17p VAT. Families and unaccompanied children taken. Camping is permitted on the farm for trekkers and a caravan may be parked there. Trekking on open moor with views of mountains and sea, on quiet sure-footed ponies. Normally the trek does not go out of a walk, but sometimes experienced riders may hold back for a canter. Bookings may be made on weekly, daily or half-daily basis. Weekly trekking £25; full day trek (including lunch) £4.50; half-day trek £2.25. Riders also taken at weekends. Open March to end of November. Well recommended for the timid person riding for the first time.

Ireland

ERRISLANNAN MANOR, Clifden, Co Galway. Tel: Clifden 27. Props: Mr and Mrs Donal Brooks. RESIDENTIAL in cottage belonging to the centre, with supervision for unaccompanied children 12–15 years old only. Hotels and guest houses nearby for older riders. All ages catered for. Riding is available every morning on reliable Connemara ponies. All rides are escorted. Guests may catch, groom, saddle and feed ponies under supervision. Ponycraft Course for young riders, Mon to Fri 10.0 am to 1.0 pm, £25 per week plus full board £15 per week. Weekly bookings only. No Sunday riding. Families from local hotels may make weekly bookings. Open for Easter and Summer school holidays only. This is a first-class centre.

Further Reading

Observer's Book of Horses & Ponies by R. S. Summerhays (Warne)

Manual of Horsemanship. British Horse Society and the Pony Club (NAC, Kenilworth)

Horses and Ponies by Judith Campbell (Hamlyn)

Pony Trekking for all by J. Kerr Hunter (Nelson)

Tschiffely's Ride by A. F. Tschiffely (Heron Books, Hodder & Stoughton)

The Romany Rye by George Borrow (Heron Books)

Black Beauty by Anna Sewell (Jarrold)

The Horse by William Youatt (1831, Longmans)

Book of the Horse, ed Brian Vesey-Fitzgerald (Nicholson & Watson)

Discovering Harness & Saddlery by G. Tylden (Shire Publications Ltd)

Horses by Roger Pocock (John Murray)

Acknowledgements

Thanks for considerable help in the preparation of this book are due to the pony breed societies, and to Anne Bell; Jane Evers-Swindell; Peggy Gilchrist, Rhydy-Croesau Riding Centre, Oswestry, Salop; Anne Harrison, Snaizeholme Riding Centre, Hawes, North Yorkshire; Ann Hyland; Hugh McGregor, Aberfoyle Centre; Ponies of Britain; Riding for the Disabled Association; Scottish Tourist Board, Edinburgh; Arthur and Evelyn Slack, Stoneriggs Trekking Centre, Hilton, Appleby, Cumbria; Jeanne Watts; Welsh Tourist Board, Cardiff; Tom Whaley; Wendy Wright; and to Penny Whaley who typed the manuscript. Additional photos came from Walter G. C. Buchanan, Glasgow; *Perthshire Advertiser; The Scotsman,* and the Misses D. M. and E. M. Alderson provided the delightful drawings.

Index

David & Charles have a book on it

The Horse's Health From A to Z by Peter D. Rossdale and Susan M. Wreford. An invaluable reference work for all concerned with the care of horses. Descriptions of diseases and conditions are followed by the recommended treatments, and drugs are listed under their chemical composition as well as under their trade names. Scientific names are cross-referenced under their common equivalents. The dictionary includes a list of veterinary associations and relevant publications, and an appendix giving British and American manufacturers. Illustrated.

Horses of the World by Daphne Machin Goodall. An illustrated record of all the breeds of horse and pony existing in the world today. 'Illustrated' is the keyword, for the author's main purpose has been to collect the best photographs available of every breed that has been photographed. Exhaustive research has gone into this collection; altogether there are some 320 pictures, 16 of them in colour, illustrating 190 breeds and types. The author has also provided a concise breed index, giving details of each breed: its locality, colours, characteristics, height, etc.

The Drove Roads of Scotland by A. R. B. Haldane. The author traces the history of the Scottish droving trade, from its origins in lawless Highland cattle thieving in the late 16th century to its position in the 19th century as the organised, large-scale movement of cattle and sheep within the commercial life of Scotland, England and the Empire itself. A classic study, blending people and the Scottish landscape into a fascinating amalgam. Illustrated.

Pit Pony Heroes by Eric Squires. A vivid and moving account of the working life of pit ponies in the Yorkshire coalfields before World War II, based on first-hand experience. Full of colourful incident and absorbing details about the workings of a pit, this is a worthy tribute to the 'pit pony heroes' whose hitherto unrecorded work has made such a contribution to the wealth of Britain. Illustrated by Ronnie Murray-Godfrey.

The Golden Guinea Book of Heavy Horses by Edward Hart. Shires, Suffolks, Percherons and Clydesdales – a comprehensive account of the part played by heavy horses throughout our history, in war and peace, their changing role and modern occupations, from forestry work to pulling brewers' drays. A full appendix tells where to see heavy horses and an illustrated glossary will prevent any confusion over technical terms. Over 70 photographs and many delightful line drawings supplement the text.

The Horse-World of London (1893) by W. J. Gordon. The horse kept the wheels of Victorian London turning; in 1893, when this book was first published, there were 300,000 in London. Within this horse world there were many ranks and degrees. The most exclusive set – the black and cream State Horses – lived at Buckingham Palace; at the bottom of the ladder was the greengrocer's drudge. In between was a great variety of horses, from the 15,000 cab horses to the massive brewers' shires. This fascinating reprint tells us how the horses of Victorian London lived, what they had to do, and who looked after them. Illustrated.

Animals as Friends by James Alldis – a headkeeper remembers London Zoo. Animals have been Jim Alldis's life; he was a zoo keeper for over 40 years, and knew and loved his charges as individuals. This warm, humorous account of animal ways – and human ways with animals – the daily round at a large zoo, the keepers and the visitors, makes delightful reading for all ages. Mr Alldis has a keen eye for fun and for eccentricities, for animals, their keepers (a bunch of real individualists, with their own tactics for dealing with tricky situations), rash children and unreasonable parents. Illustrated.

Horses, Asses and Zebras in the Wild by Colin P. Groves. A detailed description of wild horses and their relatives – their different varieties and habitats, how they live, their prospects of survival, and how many species have become extinct. The author throws new light on the origins of the domestic horse and ass, and presents a truly comprehensive picture of a fascinating subject. Illustrated.